Philadelphia

With Children

Philadelphia

With Children

Fourth Edition

A Guide to the
Delaware Valley including
Lancaster and Hershey

Elizabeth S. Gephart

Illustrated by
Candace Stringer

Camino Books, Inc.
PHILADELPHIA

Printed in Canada

3 4 5 6 7   02   01 00

Library of Congress Cataloging-in-Publication Data

Gephart, Elizabeth S., 1957-
   Philadelphia with children : a guide to the Delaware Valley / by Elizabeth S. Gephart. — 4th ed.
      p.   cm.
   Includes index.
   ISBN 0-940159-62-7
   1. Philadelphia (Pa.)—Guidebooks. 2. Family recreation—Pennsylvania—Philadelphia—Guidebooks. 3. Children—Travel—Pennsylvania—Philadelphia—Guidebooks.
   4. Philadelphia Region (Pa.)—Guidebooks. 5. Family recreation—Pennsylvania—Philadelphia Region—Guidebooks. 6. Children—Travel—Pennsylvania—Philadelphia Region—Guidebooks. I. Title.
   F158.18G47 1996
   917.48'110443—dc20   96-5985

Illustrations: Candace Stringer
Cover and interior design: Robert LeBrun

This book is available at a special discount on bulk purchases for promotional, business and educational use.

For information, write to:

Publisher
Camino Books, Inc.
P.O. Box 59026
Philadelphia, PA 19102

www.caminobooks.com

This fourth edition is dedicated to George for his encouragement and patience; to Burgo and Pater for teaching me the fun of adventure; and to Nolie, Nanny and Libby for their endless enthusiasm in exploring new places for this book.

Thanks, also, to Susanna Francies, Julia Belson and the many kind curators who helped with researching this edition.

Contents

Codes:

     ♿ *wheelchair and stroller accessibility*

     ♿ *limited wheelchair accessibility*

     ☂ *good place for a rainy day outing*

     🚌 *programs for school groups available with advance notice*

     ★ *membership benefits and discounts available*

     🎂 *birthday party facilities available with advance notice*

     🚩 *summer day camp programs available*

Handicapped and Special Services

A note from the mother of Willie, a disabled child:

Stimulation. All children need it for intellectual, physical and emotional growth. The days of the handicapped child can be filled with therapy, schooling and simply having their needs met. But seeing, feeling and smelling new things can stimulate curiosity and can make school and home lessons more significant, away from the pressures to improve.

We have seen our son, Willie, discover and enjoy a whole new world of museums, theater, music, nature and history from his wheelchair. We look for museums with plenty of hands-on activities, theaters with special wheelchair areas (discount tickets may be available), and for easy access on all outings. Repeat visits reinforce and expand the experience. The Please Touch Museum, the Schuylkill Center for Environmental Education, and the Philadelphia Zoo are extremely accessible and stimulating for our child.

Being out in the world may be your child's future, and now is the time to begin these adventures, with the security of family or friends. Even if his or her future will be a sheltered one, trips to new places and sharing different experiences can awaken new interests and create special memories.

Special Services Phone Numbers: area code (215)

Interpretive Specialist for Accessibility for Independence National Historical Park, 597-7128

Amtrak Information for the Hearing Impaired, (TTY) 1-800-523-6590

Associated Services for the Blind, 627-0600

Carousel House (Dept. of Recreation), 685-0160

Elwy-Nevil Center for Deaf and Hearing Impaired, 895-5509 or (TTY) 895-5695

Library for the Blind and Physically Handicapped, 683-3213

Mayor's Commission on People with Disabilities, 686-2798

Travel Information Service (Moss Rehabilitation Hospital), 456-9900, ext. 9603, or (TTY) 456-9602

See page 188 for a list of activities with wheelchair access.

Introduction

When I began to gather information for the first edition of *Philadelphia with Children*, the statue of William Penn on top of City Hall was the highest point in the city. Today, Penn is dwarfed by progress, and the recommended activities stretch far beyond the city limits.

As the title indicates, this book is for adventures *with* children. These can be short outings of a few hours or full days of excitement. Special sections in the back of the book can help you pick an activity. "First-Choice Activities" include some of my children's favorite places, ranging from the historic town of New Castle, Delaware to the Crayola Factory in Easton and the clever Garden State Discovery Museum in Cherry Hill, New Jersey. The Pennsylvania Renaissance Faire held in August and September is an event they also recommend highly. Other sections list free activities, locations arranged by county, and much more.

Admission times and prices are subject to change without notice. Institutions not set up for children are not listed. I apologize for any omissions or errors and would appreciate hearing any suggestions for the next edition. Please write to me care of Camino Books, P.O. Box 59026, Philadelphia, PA 19102.

The benefits of an outing with a child are immeasurable. Whether you visit a park down the street or a museum downtown, Philadelphia and the surrounding communities offer countless places to spend that special time together.

Elizabeth S. Gephart

Transportation

Many places in this book can be reached via public transportation. SEPTA offers free maps and information by phone. The Philly Phlash bus service zips around a convenient downtown loop.

Air: Philadelphia International Airport is the main airport for the city. To get to Center City, use SEPTA's airport high-speed line or drive via Route I-76 or I-95. Alternative airports are the North Philadelphia Airport or Wings Field in Blue Bell, PA.

Bus: See SEPTA below.

Car: See maps at the back of the book for major routes. Detailed maps of Philadelphia are available at the Visitors Centers at 16th Street and Kennedy Boulevard, and at 3rd and Chestnut Streets. Three bridges cross the Delaware River from Philadelphia to New Jersey: the Ben Franklin Bridge via Route I-676, the Betsy Ross Bridge off Route I-95, and the Walt Whitman Bridge via Route I-76.

PATCO (Port Authority Transit Corp.): The high-speed line runs between Philadelphia and New Jersey. Leaves from underground stop at 16th and Locust Streets or from underground stops on Market Street at 13th, 10th, and 8th Streets. Information: (215) 922-4600.

SEPTA (Southeastern PA Transit Authority): Covers the major daily routes by bus, trolley, subway, and train. Information: (215) 580-7852. Schedules and maps of routes available at SEPTA Information Center, 841 Chestnut Street, Philadelphia, Monday-Friday, 8:30 AM-4:30 PM, or at the SEPTA Customer Service and Sales Office, 15th and Market Streets, underground concourse. "Transpass" gives all-you-can-ride weekly discounts.

Subway: See SEPTA and PATCO above.

Taxi: Available from many locations.

Train: Amtrak stops at 30th Street Station (30th and Market Streets). Information: (215) 824-1600. Conrail's commuter service is run by SEPTA from all points to three Center City rail stations: 30th Street Station (30th and Market), Suburban Station (16th Street and JFK Boulevard), and Market East (Market Street between 10th and 12th Streets). Call SEPTA or your local train station for information.

Visitor Shuttle Service: PHLASH. This purple bus shuttle serves visitors throughout Philadelphia. For information, call (215) 636-1666.

History

The excitement of being right there, where America was born, is everywhere—in colonial buildings, across bumpy battlefields, and in elegant mansions preserved from earlier days.

Let the children decide which place they want to visit. Whether they're scrambling around with costumed guides in Valley Forge Park or giggling about chamber pots in colonial houses, children find unique angles from which to view our early American heritage. Perhaps the most unforgettable moment was when one of my children asked if I kept mentioning Benjamin Franklin because I knew him when I was young.

Independence National Historical Park is the best place to start with children in Philadelphia.

Independence National Historical Park

Here is an enjoyable, easy history lesson where buildings are within walking distance of each other, the open space behind the buildings along Chestnut and Walnut Streets between 2nd and 5th Streets is lovely and green, and there are plenty of benches where you can rest and talk about what you've seen. Hot dog and snack vendors make it possible to eat on-the-move.

Independence National Historical Park (INHP) in Philadelphia is the birthplace of the Declaration of Independence and of the United States Constitution.

There is no admission charge for any Park building. Hours often change depending on the season and day of the week, so it is always best to call ahead. Guides are in every open house and are knowledgeable and pleasant about answering questions. If you get tired of walking, take a horse-drawn carriage ride from one of the many parked outside Independence Hall to get a full view of the entire area. The cost of the rides depends on the length of the tour.

A special Accessibility Guide, available at the Visitor Center, tells where ramps are located. A captioned version of the film *Independence* is shown upon request. For general park information, call (215) 597-8974 (recording) or (215) 597-8975.

I recommend you start with a visit to:

Independence National Historical Park Visitor Center

3rd Street between Chestnut and Walnut Streets
Philadelphia, PA 19106
(215) 597-8974   ♿ ✞ 🚌

Hours: Daily 9 AM-5 PM. Closed Christmas and New Year's Day.

Cost: Free.

Description: If visitor centers were rated, this would win four stars. It offers free maps that are easy to read and schedules for more events than you could possibly attend. The staff people we've encountered have been invariably friendly and helpful. A large gift shop sells books and souvenirs. The film, *Independence*, and exhibits like the "Promise of Permanency" send patriotic chills through even the youngest tourist.

Betsy Ross House

Outside INHP. See Glimpses of History, page 24.

Carpenters Hall

320 Chestnut Street
Philadelphia, PA 19106
(215) 925-0167

Hours: Tuesday-Sunday, 10 AM-4 PM. Closed Tuesdays in January and February as well as Thanksgiving, Christmas, New Year's, and Easter Day.

Cost: Free.

Description: Still owned by the Carpenters Company of Philadelphia, Carpenters Hall was the meeting place of the First Continental Congress in 1774. Displays show tools and techniques used by early members who were not only skilled craftsmen but also the important architects and builders of early Philadelphia.

Congress Hall

6th and Chestnut Streets
Philadelphia, PA 19106
(215) 597-8974 (recording) or (215) 597-8975

Hours: Daily 9 AM-5 PM. Closed Christmas and New Year's Day.

Cost: Free.

Description: One of the "twin buildings" that flank Independence Hall, this is the one on the west side. It housed the U.S. Congress when Philadelphia was the capital of the United States between 1790 and 1800. Here George Washington was inaugurated for his second term and John Adams, four years later, was sworn in as President. See also Old City Hall, page 18.

Declaration House (Graff House)

7th and Market Streets
Philadelphia, PA 19106
(215) 597-5392

Hours vary.

Cost: Free.

Description: Reconstructed boarding house where Thomas Jefferson agonized over the wording of the Declaration of Independence in 1776. Short film about Jefferson.

Edgar Allan Poe National Historic Site

530 North 7th Street
Philadelphia, PA 19123
(215) 597-8780

Hours: June-October: daily 9 AM-5 PM; November-May: Wednesday-Sunday, 9 AM-5 PM.

Cost: Free.

Description: Just off the beaten path, this stark house and garden with a large raven statue convey the author's sense of mystery to teenage and adult fans. Ten-minute slide show and specialized school programs reveal the "Four Faces of Poe." January and October evening candlelight programs celebrate the author's birth and death.

> The first governor of Pennsylvania, from 1785 to 1788, was Ben Franklin.

Franklin Court

314-22 Market Street
Philadelphia, PA 19106
(215) 597-8974 (recording) or (215) 597-8975

Hours vary.

Cost: Free.

Description: Great place to exercise a child's imagination. With no plans of Franklin's house to go by, the Department of the Interior decided to build a mere outline where the house had stood. Combine this structure with domestic artifacts dug from the site and Franklin's lifestyle comes into focus. The adjacent Print Shop and Post Office remind us that he started one of the earliest newspapers and the U.S. Postal Service.

Going down the ramp and into the underground museum feels like Alice's descent into Franklinland. The Discovery Cart demonstrates Franklin's inventions to children ages 7-12. A glassed-in gallery features many Franklin inventions and push-button comments from famous people. Children love the Franklin Phone Exchange where they can hear how important people, past and present, have viewed Ben Franklin. Continuous animated doll performances of American history-in-the-making appeal to older children; younger ones have trouble with the phrasing taken from original documents of the time. An excellent movie brings the great inventor and his family to life.

Independence Hall

Chestnut Street between 5th and 6th Streets
Philadelphia, PA 19106
(215) 597-8974 (recording) or (215) 597-8975

Hours: Daily 9 AM-5 PM. Closed Christmas and New Year's Day.

Cost: Free.

Description: Originally the State House for the colony of Pennsylvania, this is where the Second Continental Congress met in 1775 and ultimately signed the Declaration of Independence on July 4, 1776. In 1787, the United States Constitution was signed in this room.

The hushed majesty of the antique furniture, green baize-covered tables, and silver ink stands with quills leave no doubt in the visitor's mind of the importance of Independence Hall. Guided tours are free but mandatory, starting in the East Wing. (Don't worry, signs point the way.)

Kosciuszko National Memorial

3rd and Pine Streets
Philadelphia, PA 19106
(215) 597-9618

Hours: Daily 9 AM-5 PM. Closed Christmas and New Year's Day.

Cost: Free.

Description: English and Polish language push-button tapes describe the famous Polish engineer Thaddeus Kosciuszko who lived in Philadelphia in 1797 and 1798. A 7-minute slide show reviews his design of West Point and other interesting accomplishments. A group portrait in the lobby pays tribute to the many foreigners, such as Lafayette and Kosciuszko, who affected the course of the American Revolution.

1,500,000 people visit Independence National Historical Park each year.

Liberty Bell Pavilion

Independence Mall
Market Street, between 5th and 6th Streets
Philadelphia, PA 19106
(215) 597-8974 (recording) or (215) 597-8975

Hours: Daily 9 AM-5 PM. Closed Christmas and New Year's.

Cost: Free.

Description: The Park Service maintains a supply of enthusiastic guides who tell the story of the Liberty Bell almost non-stop and seem pleased to answer questions from visitors. A great place to start your tour—the excitement over the significance of this single object is contagious. Liberty is, after all, what the Revolution was all about.

Lights of Liberty

PECO Energy Liberty Center
6th and Chestnut Streets
Philadelphia, PA 19106
(215) LIBERTY
www.lightsofliberty.org

Hours: May-October, nightly, dusk-11 PM. Reservations strongly recommended.

Cost: $18.00 adults, $16.00 seniors, $12.00 children 6-12, under 6 free. Discount for AAA members. $50.00 "Family 4-Pack" for two adults and two children under 12 ($10.00 for each additional child).

Description: A unique experience for kids and adults with a 60-minute, walking nighttime sound and light show depicting the events leading up to the colonists' fight for independence against the British. Pick up your 3D sound headset and follow a "Liberty Leader" to spots throughout INHP where five-story images are projected against many of the historic buildings and you "relive" many of the events. Special headsets with the Children's Channel enhance the experience for kids.

The word Pennsylvania comes from the Latin and means "Penn's Woods." The state was named in honor of William Penn's father.

New Hall Military Museum

Chestnut Street between 3rd and 4th Streets
Philadelphia, PA 19106
(215) 597-8974 (recording) or (215) 597-8975

Hours: Daily 10 AM-1 PM. Closed Christmas and New Year's.

Cost: Free.

Description: The military museum, combining the Army-Navy and Marine Corps Museums, depicts activities from the American Revolution through the last decade of the 18th century.

Old City Hall

5th and Chestnut Streets
Philadelphia, PA 19106
(215) 597-8974 (recording) or (215) 597-8975

Hours: Daily 9 AM-5 PM. Closed Christmas and New Year's.

Cost: Free.

Description: One of the "twin buildings" flanking Independence Hall, this is the one on the east side. Original City Hall for Philadelphia, home of U.S. Supreme Court, 1791-1800. Exhibits change periodically. See also Congress Hall, page 14.

Second Bank of the United States

420 Chestnut Street
Philadelphia, PA 19106
(215) 597-8974 (recording) (215) 597-8975

Hours: Daily 10 AM-5 PM. Closed Christmas and New Year's.

Cost: Free.

Description: Architect William Strickland designed this version of the Parthenon but limited the colonnades to each end. Portrait gallery inside features prominent figures in American history from 1774 to 1800.

The word Philadelphia comes from the Greek and means
"City of Brotherly Love."

Fairmount Park

Philadelphia, PA 19131
(215) 685-0000

Fairmount Park, with nearly 9000 acres, is the largest landscaped city park in the world. Its magnificent waterways and green-scapes, historic buildings, and public facilities have graced Philadelphia for the past 200 years. Site of America's centennial birthday celebration, Fairmount Park in the 1800's was beautifully landscaped and alive with activity.

Many of the historic mansions standing today in the East and West Park were originally country houses for wealthy families who lived downtown (see Park Houses, page 23). The Schuylkill River, immortalized by Thomas Eakins' oarsmen, still teems with rowing clubs. The buildings of Boathouse Row, outlined with lights after dark, provide a visual treat for children traveling along the Schuylkill Expressway or the West River Drive. Joggers, walkers, bikers, and picnic lovers dot the river banks almost all year round.

The Park provides numerous facilities where athletes congregate for formal and informal games of baseball, soccer and tennis. Swimming in the summer and sledding in the winter appeal to everyone. About 100 miles of bridle paths weave through the fields and woods for the enjoyment of both horseback riders and walkers.

Tributary creeks and their individual parks constitute nearly three-quarters of the total Fairmount Park system. Cobbs Creek Park (780 acres), Pennypack Park (1600 acres), Tacony Creek Park (250 acres), and Wissahickon Park (1700 acres) are part of a massive watershed and land preservation system, with open land, woods, footpaths, and few facilities beyond the brilliance provided by Mother Nature. Small bike path maps for each area are available through the Fairmount Park office (call 215-685-0000). To get a true feeling for the unique history swirling around each creek, look for detailed maps of these parks in local bookstores.

Andorra Natural Area

Old Northwestern Avenue, Chestnut Hill
Philadelphia, PA 19118
(215) 685-9285

Hours: Tree House, Monday-Friday, 9 AM-3 PM; Saturday-Sunday, "usually" 12 noon-4 PM.

Cost: Free.

Description: Rustic nature center welcomes children and lets them touch everything from antlers and porcupine quills to a live turtle, snake, and rabbit. Discovery Table for toddlers. Beautiful outdoor walking and bridle trails. Tree House Porch always open for all to see birds up close in nearby trees and read about them in the books provided.

Tours/Programs: Monthly program for pre-schoolers and adults. Family campfires once a month, May-September. "Unspooky Night" around Halloween.

Driving: Schuylkill Expressway to Kelly Drive West to dead end. Turn right onto Allen's Lane, follow to dead end. Turn left onto Germantown Avenue and left onto Northwestern Avenue (at Chestnut Hill College).

Historic RittenhouseTown

206 Lincoln Drive
Philadelphia, PA 19144
(215) 438-5711

Hours: Late spring-fall: Saturday-Sunday, 12 noon-4 PM. Open for school groups fall-spring: Monday-Friday, 10 AM-4 PM for papermaking (by appointment).

Cost: $4.00 adults, $2.00 children 12 and under, and seniors.

Description: A guided tour of this historic village includes seven colonial buildings and the site of America's first papermill. Try your hand at papermaking during their special workshops.

Programs/Tours: Special programs throughout the year.

Eating: Picnic tables available.

Horticulture Center

North Horticultural Drive (off Belmont Avenue)
Philadelphia, PA 19131
(215) 685-0096   ♿ ☂

Hours: Daily 9 AM-3 PM, except major and city holidays. Grounds: daily 7 AM-6 PM.

Cost: $2.00 donation.

Description: Horticulture Center stands on the grounds of the Centennial's Horticulture Hall, demolished in the 1950's. The arboretum and flower-filled greenhouses are great for lifting the spirits any time of year. The annual Pennsylvania Horticultural Society's September Harvest Show has many children's activities: competitions for the best vegetable grown over the summer, for creatures made of seeds and pods, for pumpkin painting, and more. Don't miss this low-key, uncrowded, home gardener's autumn version of the more famous Philadelphia Flower Show in March.

Japanese House and Garden

Near Horticulture Center
North Horticultural Drive (off Belmont Avenue)
Philadelphia, PA 19131
(215) 878-5097   ☂ 🚌

Hours: May-Labor Day: Tuesday-Sunday, 10 AM-4 PM. September and October: Saturday-Sunday, 11 AM-4 PM. Closed November-April.

Cost: $2.50 per person; $2.00 students and seniors.

Description: Beautiful Japanese architecture, furniture, and landscape combine to create a tranquil refuge from city life. Call for schedule of tea ceremonies and other demonstrations.

Laurel Hill Cemetery

3822 Ridge Avenue
Philadelphia, PA 19123
(215) 228-8200

Description: As daring, adventuresome outings go, this has tremendous appeal. Giant mausoleums and monuments, sculptures, and tombstones light the imagination of children of all ages. Look for the grave of Sarah Josepha Hale, who wrote "Mary Had a Little Lamb."

Memorial Hall
North Concourse Drive and Parkside Avenue
Philadelphia, PA 19131
(215) 685-0000

Description: Originally built for the Centennial celebration, this awesome building contains a replica of the Centennial fairgrounds. The Park Commission office is housed here and offers Fairmount Park information and tours by Fairmount Park Rangers.

Pennypack Environmental Center
See Nature, page 104.

Philadelphia Zoo
See Zoos, page 111.

Pennsylvania Civil War Memorial
Centennial and Lansdowne Drives
(near Memorial Hall)
Philadelphia, PA 19131

Description: The long bench flanked by tall granite towers is known to children as the "whispering bench." Try sitting at one corner of the curved stone bench and whispering a message to a friend sitting at the other corner of the bench.

Smith Memorial Playgrounds and Playhouse
Reservoir Drive near 33rd Street
Philadelphia, PA 19121
(215) 765-4325

Hours: Playhouse: Monday-Saturday, 10 AM-3:30 PM. Outdoor Playground: April-October, Monday-Saturday, 9 AM-4:45 PM; November-March, Monday-Saturday, 9 AM-4 PM. Two swimming pools open mid-June (one for ages 1-5, another for ages 6-12).

Cost: Free.

Description: It seems incredible that Mr. and Mrs. Richard Smith built this huge house and playground in 1899 just for Philadelphia's children. Giant platform sliding board, swings, and dozens of structures to climb outside. The basement of this mansion-just- for-children features cars for the very young, painted streets, stop lights, and a gas station. Other floors offer a multitude of activities for children under the age of 12.

Driving: Kelly Drive to Grant's statue. Turn onto Fountain Green Drive. Take the first right then bear right at the yield sign. Follow signs.

Park Houses

There are plenty of antiques with curious appeal for children among the fine collections: tea caddies with locks on them because tea was so valuable; long, white clay pipes for passing around after a meal—as each person took a puff, the tip was cut off before it was handed to the next.

Chamounix is the first city-owned youth hostel in the country and has hosted young people from all over the world. Strawberry Mansion's third-floor attic has doll houses and children's toys. Mount Pleasant has a child's crib attached to a canopy bed so parent and child were always together. Mount Pleasant was supposed to be the home for newly married Benedict Arnold and his wife, but he was convicted of treason before he could move in.

Woodford has our favorite collection of toys, games, knick-knacks, and handcarved Schimmel animals. The pewter "Inner and Outer Man" in the kitchen served as a hand or foot or beverage warmer in a carriage, then came inside to be a bed warmer. Holiday House Tours in December appeal to all ages.

Belmont Mansion
West Fairmount Park
(215) 878-8844

Cedar Grove
Lansdowne Drive off
North Concourse Drive
East Fairmount Park
(215) 878-2123

Chamounix Youth Hostel
North end of
West Fairmount Park
(215) 878-3676

Laurel Hill Mansion
East Edgely Drive
East Fairmount Park
(215) 235-1776

Lemon Hill
Kelly and Sedgeley Drives
East Fairmount Park
(215) 232-4337

Mount Pleasant
Mount Pleasant Drive
West Fairmount Park
(215) 763-2719

Ormiston
Ormiston Drive
East Fairmount Park
(215) 763-2222 (answers
Royal Heritage Society)

Strawberry Mansion
33rd and Dauphin Streets
East Fairmount Park
(215) 228-8364

Sweetbriar Mansion
Fairmount Park West
(215) 222-1333

Woodford Mansion
33rd and Dauphin Streets
East Fairmount Park
(215) 229-6115

Glimpses of History

Barns-Brinton House

P.O. Box 27, Route 100
Chadds Ford, PA 19317
(610) 388-1120 (weekends)
(610) 388-7376 (Chadds Ford Historical Society)

Hours: May-September: Saturday-Sunday, 12 noon-5 PM. Groups welcome anytime by appointment.

Cost: $3.00 adults, $1.00 children ages 12 and under.

Description: Guides in colonial costume explain life as it once was in this 18th-century tavern. Colonial craft demonstrations and hearth cooking. Video-taped tour available.

Driving: I-95 South, Route 322 West, then left on Route 1. House is 1 1/2 miles south of Chadds Ford.

Bartram's House and Gardens

See Gardens and Arboretums, page 90.

Betsy Ross House

239 Arch Street
Philadelphia, PA 19107
(215) 627-5343

Hours: Memorial Day-Labor Day: daily 10 AM-5 PM. Labor Day-Memorial Day: Tuesday-Saturday, 10 AM-5 PM.

Cost: Free.

Description: Seamstress Ross' colonial house is restored and set with mannequins and period furniture to give a good idea of what life was like when George Washington ordered the first American flag. Glassed-in rooms keep visitors in a one-way traffic flow along the narrow staircase. The courtyard is a nice place for weary young tourists to rest.

> Francis Chadds established a ferry service across the Brandywine River at what is now Chadds Ford.

Brandywine Battlefield State Park

P.O. Box 202, Route 1
Chadds Ford, PA 19317
(610) 459-3342   &. (*visitor center*)

Hours: Visitor Center and Houses: Tuesday-Sunday, 9 AM-5 PM; Sunday, 12 noon-5 PM. Battlefield Park grounds: September-May, Tuesday-Saturday, 9 AM-5 PM; Memorial Day-Labor Day, Tuesday-Saturday, 9 AM-8 PM; Sunday, 12 noon-8 PM.

Cost: Visitors Center and Park free. House tour: $3.50 adults, $1.50 children 6-17, under 6 free, $2.50 seniors.

Description: Permanent and rotating exhibits offer a lively education about the American Revolution. Take a tour of Washington's headquarters and Lafayette's quarters which have been reconstructed to evoke the atmosphere of the ill-fated Battle of Brandywine.

Time Needed: Minimum 1 hour.

Tours/Programs: House tours and variety of programs throughout the year. September battle reenactments in full costume delight youngsters.

Eating: Picnic tables at regular intervals in the park.

Driving: South on I-95, west on Route 322, then south on Route 1. Watch for signs on your right in the Chadds Ford area.

Brinton 1704 House

Oakland Road
Dilworthtown, PA 19380
(302) 478-2853

Hours: May-October: Saturday-Sunday, 11 AM-4 PM. Weekdays by appointment.

Cost: $3.00 per person.

Description: Authentic restoration based on the 1751 house inventories. Fancy leaded windows, indoor bake oven, raised hearth, and colonial herb garden appeal to children.

Driving: I-95 South, Route 322 West, Route 1 South, Route 100 North. At Dilworthtown, turn left onto Oakland Road and watch for house on your left.

Bucks County Covered Bridges

Bucks County Tourist Commission
152 Swamp Road
Doylestown, PA 18901
(215) 345-4552

Description: There are many stories about the invention of covered bridges, from the romantic to the practical notion of protecting animals from their natural fear of crossing over water. The Bucks County Tourist Commission offers a map to guide you on a circular tour of its 13 covered bridges.

Burlington County Historical Loops

The Burlington County Cultural and Heritage Commission
49 Rancocas Road
Mount Holly, NJ 08060
(609) 265-5068

A four-page pamphlet brings to life 28 historical buildings and Revolutionary War sites in western New Jersey. Drive your own car along the northern loop from Bordentown to Mount Holly or the southern loop from Mount Holly to Batsto.

John Chads House

P.O. Box 27, Route 100
Chadds Ford, PA 19317
(610) 388-1132 (weekends)
(610) 388-7376 (Chadds Ford Historical Society)

Hours: May-September: Saturday-Sunday, 12 noon-5 PM. Group tours available by appointment.

Cost: $5.00 adults, $3.00 children ages 6-12, under 6 free.

Description: Stone building was the home of John Chads, for whom Chadds Ford was named. Guides in colonial costume describe life in 18th-century Brandywine Valley and show how they baked in a beehive oven.

Driving: I-95 South, Route 322 West, then Route 1 South. At Chadds Ford, go right onto Route 100 North. House is a quarter mile ahead.

Delancey Street
Between Spruce and Pine, bounded by 2nd and 4th Streets
Philadelphia, PA 19106

Description: A short walk down these two blocks gives a great impression of cobblestone streets and the historic houses of Old Philadelphia. See also Elfreth's Alley and Head House Square.

Eastern State Penitentiary
Fairmount Avenue and 22nd Street
Philadelphia, PA
(215) 236-3300

Hours: May: Saturday-Sunday; June-August: Wednesday-Sunday; September-October: Saturday-Sunday, 10 AM- 5 PM; last tour 4 PM.

Cost: $7.00 adults, $5.00 seniors, $5.00 students, $3.00 children 5-17, under 5 not admitted (no exceptions).

Description: Recommended for older children and school groups only, a visit to this prison will surely make a lasting impression. It was revolutionary in its style when it opened in the early 1800's but has not been touched since it closed in 1977. The tour includes all areas open to the public, including Death Row, and focuses on the social importance of the prison over the years.

Elfreth's Alley and Museum
2nd Street between Arch and Race Streets
Philadelphia, PA 19106
(215) 574-0560

Description: Oldest continuously occupied street in America. Cobblestones and "busybodies" (mirrors by the second-floor windows for checking your neighbor's activities) are just a few of the quaint features. Number 126 is the Elfreth's Alley Museum, open 10 AM-4 PM daily. The other houses are occupied, but they are open to the public once a year, on the first weekend in June from 12 noon to 5 PM, and the first Friday night in December, 6 PM- 9 PM. Scavenger hunts for children are available at the museum.

Fort Delaware

P.O. Box 170
Delaware City, DE 19706
(302) 834-7941   &. ⌖

Hours: April-June and September, Saturday, Sunday and holidays, 11 AM-6 PM; June-Labor Day, Wednesday-Friday, 11 AM-4 PM, Saturday-Sunday, 10 AM-6 PM.

Cost: Ferry ride, Fort and Pea Patch Island: $6.00 adults, $4.00 children 2-12, under 2 free.

Description: Situated on an island in the middle of the Delaware River, this fort provides a great outing. After the one-mile ferry ride (passengers only), cross the drawbridge into the fort and spend the rest of the day exploring passageways, climbing onto the ramparts, or walking through the nature preserve at the other end of the island.

Tours/Programs: Half-hour slide show shown daily. Excellent reenactments throughout the year.

Eating: Grills, tables, and large grassy areas on island are perfect for picnics. Soft drinks, snacks, and water available at the fort.

Driving: I-95 South to Delaware Route 1 South exit. Follow Route 1 South to Route 13 South to Route 72 East. Route 72 will merge with Route 9 and lead you into Delaware City. Turn left onto Clinton Street and the parking area will be straight ahead at the bottom of the hill.

Franklin's Bust

4th and Arch Streets
Philadelphia, PA 19106

Description: Philadelphia school children donated 80,000 pennies to create this large, amiable outdoor bust of Ben Franklin.

Gazela of Philadelphia

Delaware River waterfront between Market and Lombard
Philadelphia, PA
(215) 923-9030

Description: This magnificent 106-year-old, three-masted ship welcomes visitors when she's in port. Call ahead for hours.

George Read II House and Garden

42 The Strand
New Castle, DE 19720
(302) 322-8411

Hours: Wednesday-Saturday, 10 AM-4 PM; Sunday, 12 noon-4 PM.
Last tour 3:30 PM.

Cost: $4.00 adults, $3.50 ages 12-21 and seniors, $2.00 ages 6-12,
under 6 free.

Description: Early 19th-century owner's style contrasts with
20th-century owner's taste, preserved in three rooms. Beautiful
grounds, museum shop, and tour of New Castle complete the
picture for children.

Tours/Programs: Candlelight tours and other special events.

Driving: I-95 South past Wilmington. Take Route 141 South
toward New Castle for approximately 4 miles and turn left onto
Route 9. Go over an overpass and bear right at yield sign (road
turns into Delaware Avenue). Turn left onto 2nd Street, right onto
Harmony, right onto The Strand (best to park on Delaware
Avenue and walk from there).

Germantown

See Unique Areas, page 152.

Graeme Park

859 County Line Road
Horsham, PA 19044
(215) 343-0965

Hours: Wednesday-Saturday, 10 AM-4 PM; Sunday, 12 noon-4 PM.
Last tour 3:30 PM.

Cost: $3.50 adults, $1.50 children 6-12, $3.00 seniors, under 6 free.

Description: Beautiful setting with ducks and sheep. Forty-
minute house tour emphasizes architectural form and function
such as that of the open-hearth kitchen.

Driving: PA Turnpike to exit 27 (Willow Grove). Go north on Route
611, left at County Line Road, and watch for signs on your left.

The Grange

Myrtle Avenue at Warwick Road
Havertown, PA 19083
(610) 446-4958

Hours: April-October and December, Saturday-Sunday, 1 PM-4 PM.

Cost: April-October: $2.00 adults, $1.00 children 6-18, under 6 free. December: $4.00 adults, $2.00 children 6-18, under 6 free.

Description: Mansion house, formal gardens, spring house, carriage house, summer kitchen, root cellar, and outhouse give visitors a good idea of how estates were run in the 18th and 19th centuries. Inside, children love the second-floor bureau with hidden drawers and locks. Outside, the woodland path, foot bridges, and water wheel appeal to all ages.

Driving: I-76 (Schuylkill Expressway) to City Avenue exit. Go west on City Avenue for 4 1/2 miles, go right on Earlington Road, then right on Bennington. Go just the length of two houses, watch for Grange signs and turn left on Myrtle. House is two blocks ahead, right turn through gate beyond church.

Green Hills Farm
(The Pearl S. Buck Home)

Perkasie, PA 18944
(215) 249-0100 or 1-800-220-2825

Hours: March-December: tours Tuesday-Saturday, 11 AM, 1 PM, 2 PM; Sunday, 1 PM and 2 PM. Closed Mondays, January-February, holidays and holiday weekends.

Cost: $5.00 adults, $4.00 children, $12.00 family, under 6 free.

Description: Tour the home of famous novelist Pearl Buck and see where some of her works were written. Call to find out times when a storyteller will be there to bring her children's stories alive for the audience.

Driving: PA Turnpike to exit 27 (Willow Grove), then Route 611 North into Doylestown. Go left on Route 313 North into Dublin and left on Maple Avenue. Green Hills Farm is 1 mile ahead on the right.

The state tree of Pennsylvania is the hemlock and the state flower is the mountain laurel.

Grundy Museum
610 Radcliffe Street
Bristol, PA 19007
(215) 788-9432

Hours: Monday-Friday, 1 PM-4 PM; Saturday, 1 PM-3 PM. Closed major holidays.

Cost: Free.

Description: Victorian home of Joseph R. Grundy with all its original furnishings.

Driving: PA Turnpike east to exit 29 (Delaware Valley). Go straight across the interchange to get onto Route 13 North. At the light, go right onto Green Lane, follow to the end, then go right onto Radcliffe Street. Museum is on left.

Hagley Museum and Eleutherian Mills
Route 100 at Route 141
Greenville, Wilmington, DE 19807
(302) 658-2401

Hours: January-March: open weekends, 9:30 AM-4:30 PM, guided tours Monday-Friday, 1:30 PM; March 15-December: open daily 9:30 AM-4:30 PM. Closed Thanksgiving, Christmas, and New Year's Eve Day.

Cost: $9.75 adults, $7.50 students and seniors, $3.50 children 6-14, under 6 free, $26.50 family rate.

Description: Restored powder works are just the beginning of this 19th-century industrial community. From the magnificent DuPont family residence and garden to the working water wheel to the restored millworker's house and school for mill children, there's lots to see. Flour mills in operation, 19th-century machine shop, tools and weather vane collections, Sunday school setting and more. Recommended for children ages 5 and up.

Time Needed: half day to a full day.

Tours/Programs: Tours and programs can be as detailed as your child's (or group's) interest can handle.

Eating: Picnic area, refreshments.

Driving: I-95 South to exit 7. Take Route 52 North for approximately 3 miles to Route 141 North. Follow Route 141 North for 100 yards, take first left (not marked), and follow signs to museum on left.

Hans Herr House
See Lancaster, page 165.

Head House Square and New Market
2nd Street and Pine Street
Philadelphia, PA 19147

Description: Reconstructed colonial marketplace. Programs and fairs throughout the summer months.

Hope Lodge and Mather Mill
553 Bethlehem Pike
Fort Washington, PA 19034
(215) 646-1595

Hours: Tuesday-Saturday, 9 AM-12 noon and 1 PM-4 PM; Sunday, 12 noon-4 PM.

Cost: $3.50 adults, $1.50 ages 6-12, $3.00 seniors, $8.50 family, under 6 free. Extra charge for special programs and events.

Description: Georgian mansion, gardens and grounds. Compare the lifestyles and furnishings of the original 18th-century owners with those of its 20th-century inhabitants who thought they were imitating colonial styles. Excellent children's programs let them handle reproductions of lighting devices, cooking utensils, and clothing. Young children learn and sing colonial songs while they watch a fireplace cooking demonstration. Special programs and events include Charter Day, Ballads in the Mill, Salute to Spring, and special lectures.

Driving: PA Turnpike to exit 26 (Fort Washington). Go straight after toll booths, bearing right onto Pennsylvania Avenue (not marked). At dead end, turn left onto Bethlehem Pike. Hope Lodge is three quarters of a mile ahead on left.

Masonic Temple
1 North Broad Street
Philadelphia, PA 19107
(215) 988-1917

Hours: Guided tours, Monday-Friday, 10 AM, 11 AM, 1 PM, 2 PM, 3 PM; Saturdays, 10 AM, 11 AM. Closed Saturdays, July and August.

Cost: Free.

(*continued on next page*)

Description: The Masonic Temple is to Philadelphia what the Empire State Building is to New York City: local residents keep walking around it, instead of going in. Masons meet here every night, and during the day the building is open for public tours.

Anyone with a concept of world history loves this Disneyland of architecture. Seven huge lodge halls inside represent seven different ages and architectural styles. Egyptian Hall took 12 years to create and is packed with hieroglyphics and easily recognizable symbols. Gothic Hall was built to duplicate Canterbury Cathedral with its medieval trappings.

Clever use of lighting simulates daylight outside each hall (this was the first building in Philadelphia with electricity). Masonic versatility uses pine to create marble-like statues, cast-iron stairway, plaster to resemble wood.

Massey House

P.O. Box 18
Lawrence and Springhouse Roads
Broomall, PA 19008
(610) 353-3644

Hours: April-October: Sunday, 2 PM-4:30 PM.

Cost: Donations appreciated.

Description: Tour includes house and gardens of the early English Quaker settler, Thomas Massey. Junior Guide program for children over age 11 lets them dip candles and make authentic colonial costumes while they learn all about the house and its furnishings. Junior Guides participate in programs throughout the year.

Tours/Programs: School programs by reservation.

Driving: From Philadelphia, take Market Street West onto Route 3 (West Chester Pike). Cross Route 1 (City Avenue) and go left onto Lawrence Road. Springhouse Road comes in on the right; house is on corner.

Ben Franklin and George Washington were both Masons.

Morgan Loghouse

P.O. Box 261, Wiekel Road
Kulpsville, PA 19443
(215) 368-2480   ☂ 🚌

Hours: April-December: Saturday-Sunday, 12 noon-5 PM. All year, Monday-Friday, by appointment. Tours with costumed guides. Last tour 4:30 PM.

Cost: $3.00 adults, $2.00 students and seniors, under 5 free.

Description: Originally this was a 10-room log house built in 1695 by a successful man who owned more than 800 acres. All the materials used for this house were from the property—logs, red shale, and clay. The inside of the house has a good research library and is filled with 18th-century antiques.

Tours/Programs: Follow-up outreach program free with group visit.

Eating: Picnic area by creek.

Driving: Northeast Extension of PA Turnpike to exit 31 (Lansdale). Go left onto Sumneytown Pike, then left on Troxal Road (at "Freddy's"), right on Snyder Road for one block, left on Wiekel Road to foot of hill. Morgan Loghouse is on the left across from the Township Swim Club.

Morton Homestead

100 Lincoln Avenue (Route 420)
Prospect Park, PA 19076
(610) 583-7221

Hours: April-October: Wednesday, Thursday, Saturday, 9:30 AM-3:30 PM, Friday, 9:30 AM-12:30 PM. Inside by appointment only.

Cost: Free.

Description: Earliest documented log cabin in the United States, dating back to 1650's. Built by the great-grandfather of John Morton, who signed the Declaration of Independence.

Eating: Picnic area in Governor Printz Park.

Driving: I-95 South from Philadelphia to exit 8. Follow signs to Morton Homestead.

Old Dutch House
32 East Third Street
New Castle, DE 19720
(302) 322-9168

Hours: March-December: Tuesday-Saturday, 11 AM-4 PM; Sunday, 1 PM-4 PM. January-February: Saturday, 11 AM-4 PM; Sunday, 1 PM-4 PM. Closed major holidays. Last tour at 3:30 PM.

Cost: $5.00 adults, $2.00 children 12 and under and students, $4.50 seniors.

Description: Reputed to be the oldest brick dwelling in Delaware. Tin-glazed earthenware and other collections from the Dutch Colonial period on display.

Driving: I-95 South, Route 41 South into New Castle, then left onto Route 9 which runs into Delaware Avenue. Park on Delaware Avenue. House on 3rd Street near courthouse.

Old Fort Mifflin on the Delaware
Fort Mifflin Road, near the Philadelphia Airport
Philadelphia, PA 19153
(215) 492-1881

Hours: April-November: Wednesday-Sunday, 10 AM-4 PM, tours at 1 PM and 3 PM. December-March: Monday-Friday, pre-booked group tours only.

Cost: $4.00 adults, $1.00 children 12 and under and students, $3.75 seniors.

Description: The recent renovations to the fort have made it one of the area's most interesting and unique places to visit. Everyone will love exploring from the top of the bastions overlooking the Delaware River to the underground bomb-proof casemates. The fort was the site of a siege by the British Navy in 1777, served as housing for soldiers and officers in the War of 1812, was an active prison during the Civil War, and today offers frequent demonstrations of many aspects of its history.

Tours/Programs: A variety of interactive programs and demonstrations are held throughout the summer. Guided tours usually held at 1 PM and 3 PM.

Time Needed: 1-2 hours.

Eating: Snacks available in gift shop.

Driving: South on I-95, take exit 13. Follow signs for Island Avenue. Turn left at stop sign. Follow signs for fort. (If you're coming north on I-95, take exit 10 and follow to Island Avenue. Turn right at the light, then follow signs.)

Pennsbury Manor

Route 9
Morrisville, PA 19067
(215) 946-0400   ♿ 🚌 🧍 🏳

Hours: Tuesday-Saturday, 9 AM-5 PM; Sunday, 12 noon-5 PM. Call for tour times.

Cost: $5.00 adults, $4.00 seniors, $3.00 ages 6-12, under 6 free, $13.00 family.

Description: William Penn would be thrilled to see all the activity at his country estate. Enjoy the kitchen garden, the formal garden, the livestock (sheep, a donkey, a peacock), and the beautiful Delaware River view. To better understand 17th-century life, try the brief slide show inside or take the 90-minute tour from the woodworker's shop to the smoke house to the elegant manor house. On the first Sunday in each month from April through October, interpreters in period clothing recreate aspects of 17th-century life. Usually, hands-on activities for children are included in the tour.

Tours/Programs: "Mondays at the Manor" are workshops for 4- to 6-year-olds with an adult. Good opportunities for teenage volunteers all summer. Festival Days three times a year.

Eating: Picnic pavilion.

Driving: PA Turnpike to exit 29 (Bristol). Follow Route 13 North for 2 1/2 miles. After RR station, take sharp right onto overpass (no street sign). At dead end, turn left onto Main Street. Follow Main Street (road changes names) for 2 1/2 miles to Pennsbury Memorial Road. Follow signs for Pennsbury Manor.

Penn's Landing

The activities are exciting and unique at Penn's Landing. The kids will love a visit to the new Independence Seaport Museum (see page 63), then take the Riverlink Ferry (see page 136) across the Delaware for a visit to the New Jersey State Aquarium (see page 84). You can get a pass for all three activities at any of their locations and it's the best deal in town! While you're there, watch a free family theater production (see page 117) in the open-air amphitheater, walk through the *Gazela* (see page 28) if she's in port and check the hours of RiverRink (see page 143) so you can get your skates ready.

Pennsylvania Renaissance Faire

Mount Hope Estate and Winery
Cornwall, PA 17016
(717) 665-7021

Hours: August-Labor Day: Saturday-Monday, 10 AM-6:30 PM; September-first weekend in October: Saturday and Sunday, 10:30 AM-6:30 PM

Cost: $17.95 adults, $7.00 children 5-11, under 5 free.

Description: An amazing medieval theme park complete with period costumes, jousting, juggling, storytelling, glassblowing, and much, much more. All ages will have fun while learning about every aspect of life 400 years ago.

Eating: No food or drinks are allowed to be brought in, but you can find almost anything from the 15 different food vendors.

Directions: Pennsylvania Turnpike to exit 20. Turn right onto Route 72 and follow signs for the Faire.

Pennypacker Mills

Route 73 and Haldeman Road
Schwenksville, PA 19473
(215) 287-9349

Hours: Tuesday-Saturday, 10 AM-4 PM; Sunday, 1 PM-4 PM. Closed Mondays and holidays.

Cost: Free.

Description: Visitors get a feeling for the Pennypacker family who lived here almost 100 years ago. Children are invited to touch the arrowheads and other Indian and Revolutionary War treasures collected on the property. Halloween festivals are especially geared for children.

Driving: I-76 (Schuylkill Expressway) West to Route 202. Go south on Route 202, and west on Route 422 to Collegeville. Take Route 29 North for about 8 miles, look for signs for Route 73, and turn right onto it. Pennypacker Mills is on the left immediately after you cross the bridge.

Philadelphia Vietnam Veterans Memorial
Spruce Street between Delaware Avenue and Front Street
Philadelphia, PA
(215) 564-1100

Description: Memorial to honor 642 Philadelphia residents who died during the Vietnam War.

Rock Ford Plantation
See Lancaster, page 169.

Rockwood
610 Shipley Road
Wilmington, DE 19809
(302) 761-4340

Hours: March-December: Tuesday-Saturday, 11 AM-4 PM (last tour at 3 PM); December: Sunday, 11 AM-4 PM. Closed major holidays.

Cost: $5.00 adults, $4.00 seniors, $1.00 ages 5-16, under 5 free.

Description: Rural Gothic 19th-century manor. Estate includes manor house, conservatory, carriage house, and beautiful landscaped gardens. One-hour guided tours include the room of a small boy and explanations of how children lived in 1892.

Driving: I-95 South to exit 9 (Marsh Road). Turn left onto March Road, right onto Washington Street extension. At first light, turn right onto Shipley Road. Rockwood is on the left.

Smithville
See Villages and Homesteads, page 48.

Tomb of the Unknown Soldier
Washington Square, 6th to 7th on Walnut Street
Philadelphia, PA 19105

Description: Children are fascinated by the eternal flame at the only tomb in the U.S. to honor the unknown Revolutionary War soldiers.

USS Olympia and USS Becuna
See Independence Seaport Museum, page 63.

Valley Forge National Historic Park

Valley Forge, PA 19481-0953
(610) 783-1077   🚹 🏛 🚐 (*Visitors Center and film*)

Hours: Daily, dawn to dusk. Visitors Center, daily 9 AM-5 PM. Closed Christmas Day.

Cost: Free, but some buildings have a small charge.

Description: Not a soldier's battlefield, but a field of battle between man and nature. Short movie in Visitors Center conveys the winter hardships of the Continental Army in 1778. After the film, ask for the free Children's Discovery Guide pamphlet and explore the park by foot, bike, car, or bus. Information cassettes available for rent, mid-April to October. Guides dressed in costume for special occasions add realism, fun, and stories when visitors stop at the log cabins. Local residents come on Sundays to watch radio-controlled model airplanes fly at the Park entrance near Route 202.

Time Needed: 1 hour to 1 day.

Tours/Programs: Special events/programs, reenactments throughout the year.

Eating: Picnic at Varnum's, Wayne's Woods, and Betzwood.

Driving: I-76 (Schuylkill Expressway) to exit 25. Follow North Gulph Road for 2 1/2 miles to Visitors Center on left.

Washington Crossing Historic Park

Washington Crossing, PA 18977
(215) 493-4076   🚹 🏛 🚐 🍴

Hours: Grounds: Tuesday-Sunday, 9 AM-sunset. Buildings: Tuesday-Saturday, 9 AM-5 PM, Sunday, 12 noon-5 PM.

Cost: Visitors Center free. Tour of the other buildings: $4.00 adults, $3.50 seniors and AAA members, $2.00 ages 6-12, under 6 free.

Description: Free film of Washington crossing the Delaware shown every 90 minutes in the Visitors Center. To see other buildings, you must go on the tour which leaves after each film showing. Watch a live reenactment on Christmas Day. Bowman's Hill Tower, with 121 steps, uses up lots of kid-energy (or take the elevator). Otherwise, just wander across this beautiful countryside or follow wildflower paths at Bowman's Hill Wildflower Preserve (see page 90). Call for special events including military reenactments, sheep shearing, and the candlelight tour.

(*continued on next page*)

Time Needed: Minimum 2 hours.

Eating: Picnic pavilions on the property ($1.00 parking fee).

Driving: I-95 North to New Hope exit 31, go left onto Taylorsville Road for 3 miles. Then right on Route 532, left on Route 32 (River Road). Parking on left, Visitors Center on right.

Weavertown One-Room Schoolhouse

See Lancaster, page 171.

Wheatland

See Lancaster, page 171.

Winterthur

Route 52
Winterthur, DE 19735
(302) 888-4600

Hours: Monday-Saturday, 9 AM-5 PM; Sunday, 12 noon-5 PM. We recommend making reservations in advance. Last ticket sales 3:45 PM.

Cost: Varies for different activities.

Description: Perfection everywhere. Children enjoy the 45-minute Garden Tram Tour in spring, and the Two Centuries Tour of the famous museum collection. Children not allowed on some tours. Don't miss the *KiDS! 200 Years of Childhood* exhibit through February, 2001 and the Touch-It Room, open to the public weekday afternoons and weekends. Visitors Center gift shop has whole room devoted to children's toys, books, and treasures.

Time Needed: 2 hours or more.

Tours/Programs: Period rooms by guided tour only.

Eating: Family-style restaurant in Visitors Center.

Driving: I-95 South to exit 7 (Delaware Avenue). Follow Route 52 North 6 miles to Winterthur. Or, Route 1 South, left on Route 52. Winterthur on your left.

Delaware's nicknames are the Diamond State, the First State, and the Blue Hen State.

Historical Societies and Museums

Some of the greatest treasures are kept right in our own back yard.

Historical Society of Delaware, *(302) 655-7161*
(George Read II House)

New Jersey State Historical Commission, *(609) 292-6062*
Burlington County Historical Society, (609) 386-4773
Camden County Historical Society, (609) 964-3333
Gloucester County Historical Society, (609) 845-4771

Historical Society of Pennsylvania, *(215) 732-6201*
Berks County Historical Society, (610) 375-4375
Bucks County Historical Society, (215) 345-0210
(Mercer Museum)
Chadds Ford Historical Society, (610) 388-7376
(Barns-Brinton House)
Chester County Historical Society, (610) 692-4800
(museum, library, and museum shop open to the public)
Delaware County Historical Society, (610) 359-1148
Germantown Historical Society, (215) 844-0514
Lancaster County Heritage Center, (717) 299-6440
Lehigh County Historical Society, (610) 435-1074
Marple Newtown Historical Society, (610) 353-3644
(Massey House)
Montgomery County Historical Society, (610) 272-0297
Radnor Historical Society, (610) 688-2668
(Finley House)
Valley Forge Historical Society, (610) 783-0535

Ethnic Heritage Museums
See Museums, page 74.

Religious Museums
See Historic Places of Worship, page 77.

Valley Forge got its name because of a small iron forge built along Valley Creek.

Villages and Homesteads

Living history beats schoolbooks any day. Most of the villages and homesteads let visitors try their hand at colonial chores. Children begin to understand the difference between today's pets-for-pleasure and old-time livestock (raised for food, for wool, for labor, etc.). They learn how hard work was expected from even the youngest members of these homesteads.

Compare the colonial way of life with the Amish lifestyle practiced today. Amish villages and homesteads appear in the Lancaster section, beginning on page 160.

Barclay Farmstead

209 Barclay Lane
Cherry Hill, NJ 08034
(609) 795-6225   🚐 🏮 🚩 (*Cherry Hill residents only*)

Hours: Tuesday-Friday, 9 AM-4 PM. Closed major holidays.

Cost: Free for Cherry Hill residents; $2.00 adults, $1.00 seniors and children 16 and under.

Description: Right in the midst of Cherry Hill, 32-acre farm has an operating forge barn, complete with blacksmith shop, corn crib, spring house, and restored farmhouse. Ponds and walking trails provide a nice outing.

Tours/Programs: Guided tours Tuesday and Thursday, 1 PM-3:30 PM.

Eating: Picnic tables.

Driving: Cross Ben Franklin Bridge to Route 70 East. Follow Route 70 East approximately 5 miles and take a right on Westgate Drive. Go left at the fork to Barclay Lane.

Batsto Village

4110 Nesco Road
Hammonton, NJ 08037
(609) 561-3262   ♿ 🌴

Hours: Grounds open daily, dawn to dusk. Visitors Center open daily 9 AM-4:30 PM. Mansion open for tours 10:30 AM-3:30 PM. Call ahead.

(*continued on next page*)

Cost: Mansion tour: $2.00 adults, $1.00 children 6-11, under 6 free.

Description: Deep in Wharton State Forest, Batsto Village has almost 20 buildings, well-preserved from the busy days when it forged cannons and cannon balls for the Revolutionary War. Children enjoy exploring the village with its post office, mansion, sawmill, and pens of animals.

Time Needed: Half-hour mansion tour, 2 hours to see grounds.

Eating: Summer concession stand and picnic area.

Tours/Programs: Available by advance reservation through Wharton State Forest, Batsto Visitors Center.

Driving: Benjamin Franklin Bridge to New Jersey, follow Route 30 into Hammonton. After Kessler Memorial Hospital, go left on Route 542. Follow signs for Batsto Village 7 miles ahead on left.

Colonial Pennsylvania Plantation

Ridley Creek State Park, Route 3
Media, PA 19063
(610) 566-1725

Hours: April-November: Saturday-Sunday, 10 AM-5 PM. Closed December-March. Open weekdays to school groups with reservations.

Cost: $4.00 adults, $2.00 ages 4-12 and seniors, under 4 free.

Description: Enthusiastic costumed guides, both children and adults, explain the real, often unglamorous way of life of early American farmhouses. Authentic working farm with livestock, including piglets in spring. Visitors can try spinning, making cheese, and hauling heavy buckets of water from the well. Special events regularly scheduled.

Time Needed: 1 1/2 hours to a half day.

Tours/Programs: School programs let kids do chores from candle dipping to working with animals. Good craft programs.

Eating: Picnic facilities in Park.

Driving: From Philadelphia, take I-76 (Schuylkill Expressway) to Route 476 South ("Blue Route") to Newtown Square exit. Go west on Route 3, West Chester Pike, past Newtown Square, then watch for open park on the left between Routes 252 and 352.

Conrad Weiser Homestead

28 Weiser Road
Womelsdorf, PA 19567
(610) 589-2934

Hours: Wednesday-Saturday, 9 AM-5 PM; Sunday, 12-5 PM. Closed holidays, except Memorial Day, July 4, and Labor Day.

Cost: $2.50 adults, $2.00 seniors, $1.00 children 5-12, under 5 free, $6.00 family.

Description: This was the farm of colonial Pennsylvania's famous treaty maker who kept peace with the Indians on the frontier. Visit the main house, springhouse, and gravesite amidst a beautiful 26-acre park.

Time Needed: 1-2 hours.

Eating: Picnic tables.

Driving: PA Turnpike to exit 22 (Morgantown), then north on Route 176 to Route 724 (Philadelphia Avenue). Follow Route 724 West to Route 422 West to Homestead.

Cornwall Furnace

Rexmont Road at Boyd Street, Box 251
Cornwall, PA 17016
(717) 272-9711

Hours: Tuesday-Saturday, 9 AM-5 PM; Sunday, 12 noon-5 PM. Open Memorial Day, July 4th, and Labor Day.

Cost: $3.50 adults, $3.00 seniors, $1.50 children 6-12, under 6 free.

Description: Cornwall's huge furnace produced cannons, munitions, and other iron equipment for the Revolutionary War. Watch for the giant coal bins where trains drove over the bins and dumped their load of charcoal for storage.

Time Needed: 2 hours.

Eating: Picnic tables.

Driving: PA Turnpike West to exit 20 (Lancaster), then Route 72 North to Quentin. Take a right onto Route 419 North. Iron furnace on right.

New Jersey's nickname is the Garden State.

Daniel Boone Homestead
R.D. 2, Box 162
Birdsboro, PA 19508
(610) 582-4900

Hours: Tuesday-Saturday, 9 AM-5 PM; Sunday, 12-5 PM. Closed holidays, except Memorial Day, July 4th and Labor Day.

Cost: Tour: $4.00 adults, $3.50 seniors, $2.00 children 6-12, under 6 free, $10.00 family. Grounds free.

Description: Daniel Boone spent his childhood here, learning to trap, shoot, and live in the wilderness until he left home at age 16. See the bank barn, blacksmith shop, and sawmill.

Tours/Programs: Bertolet Cabin gives organized groups of young people a chance to "rough it" overnight. Call ahead.

Time Needed: 2 hours or overnight.

Eating: Picnic areas and pavilions located throughout property. The one we liked best lies between sawmill and lodge.

Driving: I-76 West, Route 202 South to Route 422 West past Pottstown. When road is split by median strip, watch for signs and turn right on Daniel Boone Road, then left into Homestead driveway. Go past lodge to main house.

Historic Fallsington
4 Yardley Avenue
Fallsington, PA 19054
(215) 295-6567

Hours: May-October: Monday-Saturday, 10 AM-4 PM; Sunday, 1 PM-4 PM. Closed major holidays. Tour leaves every hour on the hour.

Cost: $3.50 adults, $2.50 seniors, $1.00 children 6-18, under 6 free.

Description: See how the village developed over three centuries. Go from a 17th-century log cabin to lovely 18th-century houses, to 19th-century Victorian extravaganzas. Religious life centered around four Friends meeting houses.

Time Needed: 1 hour.

Tours/Programs: Must take tour to go into buildings; see audio/visual program in headquarters.

Eating: Picnic area.

Driving: PA Turnpike east to exit 29 (Delaware Valley), north on Route 13 for 5 miles. Take the Tyburn Road West exit. Right at light onto South Main Street. Go a half mile to main building on Meetinghouse Square.

Hopewell Furnace and Village

R.D. 1, Box 345
Elverson, PA 19520
(610) 582-8773

Hours: Daily 9 AM-5 PM. Closed Thanksgiving, Christmas, and New Year's Day.

Cost: $4.00 adults, $5.00 family, under 16 free except $1.00 in summer for children 6-15.

Description: See how a 1777 iron plantation operated. Then explore the homes of the iron workers, the luxurious home of the ironmaster, the furnace, charcoal house, blacksmith's house, and cooling shed. Self-guided walking tour begins at the Visitors Center after your choice of an orientation slide show, video, or just a chat with a ranger.

Time Needed: 2 hours. Lots of walking!

Tours/Programs: Living history program in July and August with costumed blacksmiths, carpenters, and cooks at work.

Eating: Picnic tables.

Driving: PA Turnpike west to exit 23 (Morgantown). Take Route 10 South to Route 23 East to Route 345 North. Watch for signs.

Newlin Grist Mill Park

Box 219, South Cheney Road
Glen Mills, PA 19342
(610) 459-2359

Hours: Daily, dawn-dusk.

Cost: $1.50 adults, $.75 under 12, toddlers free.

Description: Most children make a beeline for the well-stocked fishing stream. Mill and miller's house, blacksmith shop, spring-house, and small log cabin reception center offer insight into the Mill's original purpose.

Eating: Picnic groves in woods and along the stream are very popular—reservations recommended.

Driving: Route 1 South through Media. Seven miles past Media, go left on South Cheney Road. Mill is on your left.

Peter Wentz Farmstead

P.O. Box 240
Worcester, PA 19490
(610) 584-5104

Hours: Tuesday-Saturday, 10 AM-4 PM; Sunday, 1-4 PM (last tour begins at 3:30 PM). Closed Mondays and major holidays.

Cost: Free, donations appreciated.

Description: Brief slide show in Peter Wentz Reception Center introduces visitors to this carefully reconstructed working farm. Livestock, growing crops, and guides in costume lend authenticity. Children love the kitchen and the children's bedroom, where blankets were warmed for the night on a special chimney ledge.

Time Needed: 1-hour house tour; allow more time for outside.

Programs: Many excellent programs where craftspeople show how to make 18th-century household items using original tools.

Driving: I-76 (Schuylkill Expressway) West, Route 202 South, to Route 422 West, to Route 363 North. Follow Route 363 North for approximately 10 miles. Turn right onto Skippack Pike and watch for signs.

Pusey House and Landingford Plantation

15 Race Street
Upland, PA 19015
(610) 874-5665

Hours: May-October: Saturday and Sunday, 1 PM-4 PM, or by appointment.

Cost: $1.00 adults, $.75 children and students, or a donation.

Description: Caleb Pusey's house was built in 1683 and has been preserved in its original condition. See large kettle (probably used to dye clothes or brew beer), beehive oven, the well inside the house, and a candlestock used for candles or for removing pig bristles after the animals were slaughtered.

Driving: I-95 South to Widener University exit in Chester. Turn right off ramp, then left onto 14th Street, which turns into Upland Avenue. Pass Crozer-Chester Medical Center on Upland, turn right on 6th, then left on Main. Follow bend which leads to Race Street.

Smithville

P.O. Box 6000
Smithville Road
Easthampton, NJ 08060
(609) 265-5068   ♿ 🚐 🏛

Hours: April-October: Wednesday and Sunday, 1 PM, 2 PM, 3 PM.

Cost: $5.00 adults, $3.00 students, $4.00 seniors, under 6 free.

Description: This town was so complete it even had, in 1892, a bicycle commuter railway connecting it to nearby Mount Holly (the H.G. Smith Company invented a kerosene-burning tricycle and the high-wheeled Star bicycle). In the 1840 mansion, see children's room, doll collection, and children's tram.

Time Needed: 1 hour for tour.

Tours/Programs: Tour features Orientation/Exhibit Center, Victorian House Museum, Casino Annex/Art Gallery, gardens and grounds. Guides can adjust tour for children.

Driving: From Philadelphia, take the Benjamin Franklin Bridge to Route 70 East to Route 38 East to Smithville Road. Go left on Smithville Road, then watch for the mansion on your left (Route 206 is too far).

Wheaton Village

Millville, NJ 08032
(609) 825-6800 or 800-998-4552   ♿ 🍴 🏛

Hours: April-December: daily 10 AM-5 PM; January-March: Wednesday-Sunday, 10 AM-5 PM. Closed major holidays.

Cost: $7.00 adults, $3.50 ages 6-18, under 6 free, $6.00 seniors, $12.00 family. Reduced winter rates.

Description: Watch glass blowers at work in 1888 glass factory still in full use. Museum of American Glass has more than 7500 pieces. Half-scale railroad takes visitors on a three-quarter-mile trip around Village grounds. Youngest children enjoy playground and lakeside. Older ones watch tinsmiths at work and demonstrations of pottery, woodworking, and glass lamp working. Visit the new Down Jersey Folklife Center and be sure to bring lots of pennies for the penny candy in the general store!

Time Needed: 2 hours.

Tours/Programs: Glass blowing demonstrations at 11 AM, 1:30 PM, and 3:30 PM. Artists' demonstrations and special events throughout the year.

(*continued on next page*)

Eating: Country Inn and Country Kitchen adjacent to grounds.

Driving: Cross Ben Franklin or Walt Whitman Bridge from Philadelphia into New Jersey to I-676 South, to Route 42 South, to Route 55 South (it all happens quickly). Stay on Route 55 to exit 26. Follow the brown Wheaton Village signs to the main entrance.

Camden was originally named Cooper's Ferry after ferry operator William Cooper.

The Benjamin Franklin Bridge took four years to construct and used 15,000 gallons of paint, 61,700 tons of steel and 618 lights.

Museums

Train museums, doll museums, soldier and war museums, natural history museums, art and science museums, even a Mummers museum—there are enough in this area to delight a child with a different museum every weekend for almost two full years! Interactive museums are included here too—don't miss the Crayola Factory in Easton and the Garden State Discovery Museum in Cherry Hill.

A number of outstanding museums are not listed out of respect for their exclusivity. The Barnes Foundation art collection, for instance, is one of my favorite museums, but since it does not admit children under 12 years old, it is not included here.

Collections

Academy of Natural Sciences

19th Street and the Parkway
Philadelphia, PA 19103
(215) 299-1000

Hours: Monday-Friday, 10 AM-4:30 PM; Saturday, Sunday and some holidays, 10 AM-5 PM. Closed Thanksgiving, Christmas, and New Year's Day.

Cost: $8.50 adults, $7.75 seniors, $7.50 children 3-12, under 3 and members free.

Description: Home of everyone's favorite full-scale roaring dinosaur. "Discovering Dinosaurs" is an exciting, multi-media approach to the beasts with lots of games to play and buttons to push. Be sure to try your hands at an archaeological "dig" and look for fossils. "Outside-In" is the museum's special third-floor children's nature area where they can explore habitats, play with small animals, and stay busy. Intriguing dioramas.

Time Needed: 2 hours.

Tours/Programs: Outstanding programs using live animals help children ages 3 and over better understand the animal kingdom.

Eating: "Dino Diner" has tables and vending machines.

Allentown Art Museum

31 North Fifth Street
P.O. Box 388
Allentown, PA 18105
(610) 432-4333

Hours: Tuesday-Saturday, 11 AM-5 PM; Sunday, 12 noon-5 PM.

Cost: $4.00 adults, $3.00 seniors, children 12 and under free. Sundays, all free.

Description: Small and friendly—a great art museum for children. Visit the Interactive Learning Center with hands-on art activities and be sure to ask for the Kids Treasure Hunt pamphlet at the front desk. Older children enjoy the Frank Lloyd Wright Room and a chance to search for his red trademark.

Tours/Programs: Many children's programs through the year,

(*continued on next page*)

including Art Smart every month and Art Time, a hands-on program, on Sundays, 12 noon-3 PM and Tuesdays and Thursdays, 3 PM-4:30 PM.

Driving: PA Turnpike to the Northeast Extension to exit 33 (Lehigh Valley). Follow Route 22 East to 7th Street. Turn right on 7th, left on Turner Street for two blocks, then right onto 5th. Museum is 1 1/2 blocks ahead on the left, behind the courthouse.

American Helicopter Museum

1220 American Boulevard
Brandywine Airport
West Chester, PA 19380
(610) 436-9600
www.helicoptermuseum.org

Hours: Wednesday-Saturday, 10 AM-5 PM; Sunday, 12 noon-5 PM. Monday and Tuesday by appointment only.

Cost: $5.00 adults, $3.50 children.

Description: Several hands-on exhibits, a working wind tunnel, several video presentations, and a theater presentation make this a fun place to learn about helicopters and the science behind their flight. Children can sit in the cockpit of an actual helicopter and look at over 40 exhibits, including the V-22 Osprey (a cross between an airplane and a helicopter). An individual guide who incorporates science, engineering, and history into a great presentation gives all visitors a tour.

Time Needed: 1 hour.

Driving: Route 76 West to Route 202 South toward West Chester. Go approximately 10 miles to the Boot Road exit. Turn left onto Boot Road. At third light, turn right onto Wilson Drive. Go 1/4 mile and turn left onto Airport Road. Make a right onto American Blvd., pass helicopter, turn left, and look for red awning.

Atwater Kent Museum

15 South 7th Street
Philadelphia, PA 19106
(215) 922-3031

Hours: Daily 10 AM-5 PM. Closed Tuesdays.

Cost: $3.00 adults, $1.50 ages 3-12, under 3 free, $2.00 seniors.

(*continued on next page*)

Description: Treasures and trivia of old Philadelphia abound. Artifacts, maps, paintings, prints, and photographs reflect the city's social and cultural history.

Balch Institute

See Ethnic Heritage Museums, page 74.

Boyertown Museum of Historic Vehicles

28 Warwick Street
Boyertown, PA 19512
(610) 367-2090

Hours: Tuesday-Sunday, 9:30 AM-4 PM. Closed most major holidays.

Cost: $4.00 adults, $3.50 seniors, $2.00 children 6-18, under 6 free.

Description: Here you can see more than 100 different vehicles from old sleighs to butcher's wagons to high-wheel bicycles—all built in southeastern Pennsylvania. Careful preservation of the Boyertown-to-Reading stagecoach, old fire equipment, and several of Charles Duryea's Reading automobiles reveal a deep interest and pride in local heritage.

Driving: I-76 (Schuylkill Expressway) West to Route 202 South and quickly onto Route 422 West to Route 100 North at Pottstown, to Boyertown exit. Go left onto Route 73. At 5th light, turn left onto Reading Avenue. At the fork, go straight (road bears to the right). Museum parking lot ahead on the left.

Brandywine River Museum and Conservancy

Route 1
Chadds Ford, PA 19317
(610) 388-2700

Hours: Daily 9:30 AM-4:30 PM. Closed Christmas Day.

Cost: $5.00 adults, $2.50 ages 6-18, under 6 free.

Description: An indoor-outdoor museum, focusing on the beautiful Brandywine Valley and the museum's adjacent nature preserve. Old grist mill museum displays paintings by the Wyeths and their compatriots. Rugged book illustrations appeal to older children who know the stories of Robin Hood, Treasure Island, etc. Even the youngest children love the cobblestone courtyard and the inside ramps.

Time Needed: 1 1/2 hours.

(*continued on next page*)

Tours/Programs: Children of all ages love the annual holiday train display and the giant Christmas trees decorated with natural materials from the surrounding woods and fields. Interesting programs and shows all year round. Free family fun day in summer.

Eating: Restaurant in museum.

Driving: I-95 South to Route 322 West to Route 1 South. After crossing Route 100 in Chadds Ford, watch for museum on left.

Childventure Museum

430 Virginia Drive
Fort Washington, PA 19034
(215) 643-3233 or 643-9906

Hours: Tuesday-Saturday, 10 AM-4 PM; Sunday, 12 noon-4 PM.

Cost: $4.00 per person.

Description: Child's museum and prominent gift shop offer plenty to see and do. Creative play spaces encourage young children to use their imagination; museum exhibits appeal to all ages.

Driving: PA Turnpike to exit 26 (Fort Washington). Turn right at first light to Commerce Street. At first stop sign, turn right. Museum is third building on left.

Choo-Choo Barn

See Lancaster, page 162.

Civil War Library and Museum

1805 Pine Street
Philadelphia, PA 19103
(215) 735-8196

(Steep townhouse stairs make the building inaccessible
for wheeled vehicles of any sort.)

Hours: Tuesday-Saturday, 10 AM-4 PM.

Cost: $5.00 adults, $3.00 children 4-12, under 4 free.

Description: Civil War documents and treasures, many donated by their original owners. Drummer Boy exhibit extols the importance of those patriotic young communicators.

(continued on next page)

Time Needed: 1 hour.

Tours/Programs: Personal guided tours on several levels depending upon visitors' knowledge of the period.

Colonial Flying Corps Museum
New Garden Aviation, Newark Road
Toughkenamon, PA 19374
(610) 268-8988

Hours: Call ahead for hours, or by appointment.

Cost: $1.00 adults, $.50 children.

Description: Small but interesting collection of antique airplanes, motorcycles and cars. Someone always on duty to answer questions about classics such as 1929 DuPont auto, Indian motorcycles from 1907 to 1952, Staggerwing Beech and Grumman Wildcat planes.

Eating: Picnic tables, snack bar in airport.

Driving: I-95 South to Route 322 West to Route 1 South to Kennett Square Bypass to Toughkenamon exit. Go left onto Newark Road. Museum is 2 miles ahead on the right.

Crayola Factory at Two Rivers Landing
P.O. Box 431
Easton, PA 18044
(610) 515-8000

Hours: Daily 9:30 AM-4 PM. Closed on New Year's Day, Easter, Thanksgiving, and Christmas.

Cost: $6.00 adults and children, $5.50 seniors, under 2 free.

Description: An exciting attraction where you can watch how Crayola crayons and markers are made (and get free samples) plus spend several hours exploring all the interactive activities. Where else can you color on the walls, climb through a Media Maze, and discover art through science experiments? They even provide you with your own bag to take home all the goodies you create.

Eating: Restaurant on first floor of building where you can eat as a family or reserve a room for a large group. Other restaurants nearby in Easton.

Driving: Pennsylvania Turnpike to Northeast Extension (Route 9) to exit 33. Follow Route 22 East to 4th Street exit. Follow signs for Crayola Factory.

Delaware Agricultural Museum

866 North DuPont Highway (Route 13)
Dover, DE 19901
(302) 734-1618

Hours: April to mid-December: Tuesday-Saturday, 10 AM-4 PM; Sunday, 1-4 PM. Open to groups all year by appointment.

Cost: $3.00 adults, $2.00 ages 6-18 and seniors, under 6 free.

Description: Lots to see! The main exhibit space has agricultural equipment, displays, and special kids' exhibits. A historic 19th-century village recreates the rural agricultural tradition. Watch for the poultry exhibit inside and live animals outside.

Tours/Programs: Scheduled weekend activities include Springtime on the Farm (with sheep shearing), Fall Harvest Festival, and a Farmer's Christmas.

Driving: I-95 South to Route 13 toward Dover, DE. Watch for Museum just south of Delaware State College and Dover Mall.

Delaware Art Museum

2301 Kentmere Parkway
Wilmington, DE 19806
(302) 571-9590

Hours: Tuesday-Saturday, 9 AM-4 PM; Wednesday, 9 AM-9 PM; Sunday, 12 noon-4 PM. Closed Thanksgiving, Christmas, and New Year's Day.

Cost: $5.00 adults, $3.00 seniors, $2.50 students, 6 and under free. Saturday, 9 AM-12 noon, all free.

Description: "Pegofoamasaurus" Children's Gallery starts with welcoming doors for every size person. Peg-covered walls for children to create their own art with infinitely different shapes and colors of foam. Check ahead on weekdays so your visit won't conflict with school groups.

Eating: Field next to parking lot is good for picnics.

Driving: I-95 South to Route 52 Delaware Avenue exit 7. Go right at the first light onto Pennsylvania Avenue. Bear right where the road splits. Go 2 miles, then right onto Bancroft Parkway to dead end. Go left onto Kentmere Parkway. Museum is on right.

Delaware Museum of Natural History

P.O. Box 3937
Wilmington, DE 19807
(302) 652-7600 recorded, or 658-9111

Hours: Monday-Saturday, 9:30 AM-4:30 PM; Sunday, 12 noon-4:30 PM. Closed July 4th, Thanksgiving, Christmas, and New Year's Day.

Cost: $5.00 adults, $3.00 ages 3-17, under 3 free, $4.00 seniors.

Description: Here you truly float through land, water, and air. "Land" exhibit focuses on mammals found in Delaware. "Water" uses incredible shell collection and treasures to recreate the Great Barrier Reef. In "Air," watch for those huge birds of prey perched above you in the trees.

Time Needed: 2 hours.

Tours/Programs: Newly renovated Discovery Room, open on weekends and for special events, has many hands-on activities. Weekend workshops presented all year round. Spring and winter Children's Weeks offer special events. Halloween festival.

Driving: I-95 South from Philadelphia to exit 7 (Delaware Avenue). Take Route 52 North. Museum is 5 miles ahead on the left.

Delaware Toy and Miniature Museum

P.O. Box 4053
Route 141
Wilmington, DE 19807
(302) 427-TOYS (8697)   *(with advance notice)*

Hours: Tuesday-Saturday, 10 AM-4 PM; Sunday, 12 PM-4 PM. Closed Monday.

Cost: $5.00 adults, $4.00 seniors, $3.00 children ages 12 and under.

Description: Great appeal for anyone who appreciates miniatures and doll houses of all kinds. See grand Victorian homes, manor houses complete with armor, stables and even Noah's Arks. Special tea parties held several times a year.

Directions: I-95 South to exit 7 (Delaware Avenue) to Route 52 North to Route 100 North to Route 141 North. Follow signs to the Delaware Toy and Miniature Museum and Hagley Museum.

Discover Lancaster County History Museum
See Lancaster, page 163.

Elfreth's Alley Museum
See Glimpses of History, page 27.

Fireman's Hall Museum
Second and Quarry Streets
Philadelphia, PA 19106
(215) 923-1438

Hours: Tuesday-Saturday, 9 AM-4:30 PM. Closed major holidays.

Cost: Free. Donations requested.

Description: The authentic 1815 hand pumper appeals to the imagination, but young minds find earlier firefighting equipment totally incredible. Hand-sewn leather buckets and crude hatchets don't look like much until they're seen in pictures of community bucket brigades. Ben Franklin started the first fire company in 1736. Equipment through the ages, firemarks, and the recreated firemen's living quarters give visitors plenty to see.

Folk Craft Center and Museum
See Lancaster, page 164.

Fonthill Museum
East Court Street
Doylestown, PA 18901
(215) 348-9461

Hours: Monday-Saturday, 10 AM-5 PM; Sunday, 12 noon-5 PM. Last tour at 4 PM. Make reservations ahead. Closed Thanksgiving, Christmas, and New Year's Day.

Cost: $5.00 adults, $4.50 seniors, $1.50 students 6-17, under 6 free.

Description: Henry Mercer built Fonthill for his collection of prints and tiles from around the world. Even children with no interest in ceramics are fascinated by the medieval castle-like atmosphere of this very unusual house. Further down the driveway, visit Mercer's Moravian Pottery and Tile Works (page 177) and the nearby Mercer Museum (page 65).

(*continued on next page*)

Tours/Programs: We recommend the Tower Tour for families, 10:30 AM-11:30 AM on the first Saturday of each month. Reservations required—call the day before the tour to reserve a spot.

Eating: Picnic area in Fonthill Park.

Driving: PA Turnpike to exit 27 (Willow Grove). Follow Route 611 North through Doylestown, and turn right on East Court Street. Watch for signs.

Franklin Institute

20th Street and Ben Franklin Parkway
Philadelphia, PA 19103
(215) 448-1200

Hours: Opens daily at 9:30 AM. Closes Monday-Wednesday at 5 PM. Future Center and Theater open Thursday-Saturday until 9 PM, Science Center open until 5 PM. Future and Science Centers and Theater open Sunday, 9:30 AM-6 PM. Fels Planetarium—call for hours.

Cost: Science Center and Future Center: $9.75 adults, $8.50 children ages 4-11 and seniors. Centers and Omniverse Theater: $12.00 adults, $10.50 children ages 4-11 and seniors. Theater only (available Thursday-Saturday, 4 PM-9 PM only): $7.00 adults, $6.00 children ages 4-11 and seniors, children under 4 free.

Description: Dynamic preview of future science and future life. The Mandell Future Center uses state-of-the-art computer capabilities to create exciting interactive exhibits where kids can "drive a car," rearrange their faces by computer, play computer music in a jamming room, check out clothes made of tomorrow's materials, and much, much more. The Tuttleman Omniverse Theater shows a giant 79-foot-wide screen with 56 speakers and enough action to make you feel you're right there. And don't leave without taking a walk through the heart!

Time Needed: 2 hours to a full day.

Tours/Programs: Frequent programs throughout the year. Flashlight Holiday concert in December.

Eating: Three cafeterias with a variety of food for kids and adults; picnic tables inside and outside.

Delaware was named for Virginia's governor, Thomas West, Lord de la Warr.

Franklin Museum

Route 1, Baltimore Pike
Franklin Center, PA 19063
(610) 459-6168

Hours: Monday-Saturday, 9:30 AM-4:30 PM; Sunday, 1 PM-4:30 PM. Closed holidays.

Cost: Free.

Description: Large, well-designed display of pewter, bronze, coins, porcelain, and collectibles.

Driving: Route 1 South from Philadelphia. After Media, watch for Franklin Center on your left.

Free Library of Philadelphia

Logan Square
Philadelphia, PA 19103
(215) 686-5322

Hours: Monday-Wednesday, 9 AM-9 PM; Thursday-Friday, 9 AM-6 PM; Saturday, 9 AM-5 PM; Sunday, 1 PM-5 PM. Closed Sundays in the summer.

Cost: Free.

Description: Philadelphia's largest collection of books for children and for those studying children's literature. Also records, tapes, magazines, foreign language books, story hours, and vacation reading clubs. Volunteers available to take reading materials to homebound readers: call (215) 686-5411.

Garden State Discovery Museum

16 North Springdale Road
Cherry Hill, NJ 08003
(609) 424-1233

Hours: Tuesday-Sunday, 9:30 AM-5:30 PM. July and August: open Thursday until 8:30 PM. September-June: open Saturday until 8:30 PM. Closed Mondays (except Monday holidays), Thanksgiving, and Christmas.

(*continued on next page*)

Cost: $6.95 per person, $5.95 seniors, children under 1 free.

Description: An outstanding new museum, which children 10 and under will not want to leave. They can help build a house, sail a boat, become a cook and waiter at a diner (with such fare as hamburgers and sushi), practice rock climbing, add materials to an ongoing woven rug, be a vet and examine some real animal x-rays, find a way through a giant spider web without ringing the bells attached to some of the strings, or encase their entire body in a giant bubble.

Time Needed: 2 hours.

Tours/Programs: Special events almost every weekend with different themes each month. Don't miss multi-cultural month of January. After-school program available. May children's festival.

Eating: Vending machines for drinks and snacks, indoor and outdoor picnic area.

Glencairn Museum

1001 Cathedral Road
Box 757
Bryn Athyn, PA 19009
(215) 938-2600

Hours: Monday-Friday, 9 AM-4 PM by reservation only for tours. Open without tours second Sunday of every month, 2 PM-5 PM, except July and August.

Cost: $4.00 adults, $3.00 seniors, $2.00 students, 12 and under free.

Description: Young history students have plenty to see in this unusual collection of art and objects arranged in galleries by subject, including Greece and Rome, Near East and Far East, Middle Ages, Native American and French art.

Tours/Programs: 2-hour guided tour. Call for information about concerts held in Great Hall.

Driving: Directions given with reservations.

Hall of Fame Sports Museum

See Bridgeton, page 149.

Hands-on House
See Lancaster, page 165.

Hershey Museum
See Hershey, page 158.

Historic Burlington County Prison-Museum

128 High Street
Mount Holly, NJ 08060
(609) 518-7667

Hours: Call for hours.

Cost: Free, donations appreciated.

Description: This prison, where both a Supreme Court justice and the Boston Strangler have been jailed, was built in 1811 and used until 1965. One-hour tour explains its history and includes some exciting stories of prison life. See their cells, each with fireplace and window. The "dungeon" is said to be haunted! First fireproof building in the U.S.

Driving: Ben Franklin Bridge to New Jersey, I-295 North to Mt. Holly exit. Follow Route 38 East to Mt. Holly Bypass (Route 541 North), go right at first light, left at second light onto High Street. Museum is 1 1/2 blocks on the right.

Independence Seaport Museum

Penn's Landing at
211 South Columbus Blvd. and Walnut Street
Philadelphia, PA 19106-1415
(215) 925-5439

Hours: Daily 10 AM-5 PM. Closed Thanksgiving and Christmas.

Cost: Museum only: $5.00 adults, $4.00 seniors, $2.50 ages 5-12, under 5 free. Museum and Historic Ship Zone: $7.50 adults, $6.00 seniors, $3.50 ages 5-12, under 5 free. Riverpass (Museum, Historic Ships, New Jersey State Aquarium, Riverbus Ferry): $15.00 adults, $12.00 seniors, $10.00 ages 3-12, under 3 free.

Description: All the fine maritime resources at Penn's Landing have joined forces to provide an exciting seaport experience. Walk through historic old ships, the *U.S.S. Olympia* and *U.S.S. Becuna,* visit a boat-building workshop, explore the Independence Seaport Museum with its interactive exhibits, films, and special programs. Journey beneath the sea with "Divers of the Deep."

Time Needed: 1-2 hours.

Tours/Programs: Many programs throughout the year.

Institute of Contemporary Art

The University of Pennsylvania
118 South 36th Street
Philadelphia, PA 19104
(215) 898-7108

Hours: Wednesday-Friday, 12 noon-8 PM; Saturday-Sunday, 11 AM-5 PM.

Cost: $3.00 adults, $2.00 seniors, artists, and students. Free on Sunday, 10 AM-12 noon. Children 12 and under free.

Description: Four major exhibits shown during the school year. Workshops for 5- to 12-year-olds every weekend during the school year.

James A. Michener Art Museum

138 South Pine Street
Doylestown, PA 18901
(215) 340-9800

Hours: Tuesday-Friday, 10 AM-4:30 PM (Wednesday until 9 PM); Saturday-Sunday, 10 AM-5 PM.

Cost: $5.00 adults, $4.50 seniors, $1.50 students.

Description: Housed in an old prison, this museum has three permanent collections and hosts many traveling exhibits. Look for familiar Bucks County scenes in the Visual Heritage Exhibit, recognize local artists (of all kinds) in the Creative Bucks County display, and watch the kids' reactions to the fascinating Nakashima furniture. Many special events and workshops for all ages throughout the year.

Driving: PA Turnpike to exit 27 (Willow Grove). Follow 611 North (about 20 minutes) through Doylestown (do not take bypass). Turn right at light onto Ashland Street. Go one block, turn right onto Pine Street. Park in library parking lot next to museum.

Library for the Blind and Physically Handicapped

919 Walnut Street
Philadelphia, PA 19106
(215) 925-3213

Description: Mail-order service offers large collection of large-print books, talking books, cassette books, braille books, and periodicals.

Mary Merritt Doll Museum and Merritt's Museum of Childhood

843 Benjamin Franklin Highway (Route 422)
Douglassville, PA 19518
(610) 385-3809 (Doll Museum)
(610) 385-3408 (Museum of Childhood)

Hours: Monday-Saturday, 10 AM-5 PM; Sunday, 1 PM-5 PM. Closed Tuesdays and major holidays.

Cost: $3.00 adults, $1.50 children 5-12, under 5 free. Admission to both museums included in price. No admission cost for doll shop.

Description: The Doll Museum: great collection of dolls, doll houses, Noah's Arks. Museum of Childhood: one-room exhibit of childhood mementos, doll houses, banks, American Indian artifacts, sleighs, costumes, and a full-sized handcarved canoe.

(*continued on next page*)

Driving: I-76 (Schuylkill Expressway) West to Route 202 South to Route 422 West. Museum on the right beyond Pottstown.

Mercer Mile

See Mercer Museum, below; Fonthill, page 58;
Moravian Pottery and Tile Works, page 177.

Mercer Museum and Spruance Library

Pine and Ashland Streets
Doylestown, PA 18901
(215) 345-0210

Hours: Monday-Saturday, 10 AM-5 PM; Sunday, 12 noon-5 PM; Tuesday, 10 AM-9 PM. Closed Thanksgiving, Christmas Day, and New Year's Day.

Cost: $5.00 adults, $4.50 seniors, $1.50 ages 6-17, under 6 free.

Description: Intriguing castle-like museum with displays that you walk over, under, and around. Tools used by early Americans range from beehive oven to gallows. Discover a hurdy-gurdy, a cloverheader, a snairing, and a sausage stuffer. See an old school and the shops of a hatter, baker, lumberman, basket and broom maker. Clock making, gun smithing, glass blowing.

Time Needed: 2 hours to a full day.

Tours/Programs: Many fun programs throughout the year.

Driving: PA Turnpike to exit 27 (Willow Grove), then Route 611 North to Doylestown. Cross Route 202; at light, take a *sharp* right on Green Street. Museum is on the left.

Mummers Museum

2nd Street and Washington Avenue
Philadelphia, PA 19147
(215) 336-3050

Hours: Tuesday-Saturday, 9:30 AM-5 PM; Sunday, 12 noon-5 PM. Closed Mondays, Thanksgiving, Christmas, and New Year's Day. Closed Sundays in July and August.

Cost: $2.50 adults; $2.00 children, seniors, and students.

Description: Just as much fun as the famous Mummers Parade! Full of sights and sounds to get feet moving, including video instructions on how to do the Mummers Strut.

Time Needed: 1 hour

Mutter Museum of the College of Physicians

19 South 22nd Street
Philadelphia, PA 19103
(215) 587-9919

Hours: Tuesday-Saturday, 10 AM-4 PM.

Cost: $8.00 adults, $4.00 children, students, and seniors.

Description: Skeletons and old medical equipment are just a few of the items in the history of medicine and treatment center.

Nail House Museum

See Bridgeton, page 150.

New Jersey State Museum and Planetarium

205 West State Street
Trenton, NJ 08608
(609) 292-6308

Hours: Tuesday-Saturday, 9 AM-4:45 PM; Sunday, 12 noon-5 PM. Closed major holidays and Mondays. Planetarium shows: Saturday and Sunday, 1 PM, 2 PM, 3 PM; July and August weekday shows—call for times.

Cost: Free ($1.00 per person for planetarium).

Description: Everything under one roof, including the planetarium and Delaware Valley Indian displays. See North American mammals, reptiles, and the Hadrosaurus, "first dinosaur in North America, found in Haddonfield, NJ... hence, the name." Hall of Natural Science shows how the earth has evolved from the solar system, 4.5 billion years ago, to the present—and how it might be in the future. Also galleries of paintings, sculpture, and other arts.

Time Needed: 2 hours to a half day.

Driving: Ben Franklin Bridge to New Jersey, follow signs to I-295 North to Route 130 North to Route 206 North. Left on Laylor Street to Route 29. Go right on Route 29 to Calhoun Street. At exit ramp light, turn right onto West State Street. Museum is second building on the right.

New Jersey is the most densely populated state in the Union. Both Princeton and Trenton have been, briefly, the country's capital city.

North Museum of Franklin and Marshall College

See Lancaster, page 167.

Old Barracks Museum

Barrack Street
Trenton, NJ 08608
(609) 396-1776

Hours: Daily 10 AM-5 PM. Closed major holidays.

Cost: $6.00 adults, $3.00 seniors and students.

Description: There are only five wartime barracks left in the United States. This was built to house soldiers during the French and Indian Wars (1689-1763). If you're curious, talk to some of the soldiers about their life there; role-playing guides make the difficulties of barracks life very clear. In all, 300 men plus women and children lived together here. The women were allowed half-rations for themselves and their children, in exchange for cooking, cleaning, and sewing. Complete renovation finished in 1997. Interactive lab. Modern exhibit gallery.

Driving: Go across any bridge to I-95 North to Route 1 North through toll bridge to first exit in New Jersey, Route 29 Gatehouse complex exit. Take Route 29 North to Willow Street exit. At light, go straight into Museum parking lot.

Pennsylvania Academy of the Fine Arts

Broad and Cherry Streets
Philadelphia, PA 19102
(215) 972-7600

Hours: Monday-Saturday, 10 AM-5 PM; Sunday, 11 AM-5 PM.

Cost: $5.00 adults, $4.00 students and seniors, $3.00 children ages 5-18, under 5 free.

Description: The combination of museum and school makes a visit here an enjoyable learning experience. Manageable size with changing exhibits from the Academy's outstanding American collection. Look at the building from the outside, too!

Tours/Programs: Family programs once a month.

Pennsylvania Hospital and Nursing Museum

8th and Spruce Streets
Philadelphia, PA 19107
(215) 829-7354 (medical library)

Hours: Monday-Friday, 8:30 AM-5 PM.

Cost: Free. Go to Marketing Office, 2nd floor of Pine Building, for admission.

Description: Call ahead for tour which includes history of hospital, early medical instruments, history of Nursing Museum, and the nation's first surgical amphitheater (built 1804).

Philadelphia Museum of Art

26th Street and Ben Franklin Parkway
P.O. Box 7646
Philadelphia, PA 19101
(215) 763-8100

Hours: Tuesday-Sunday, 10 AM-5 PM; Wednesday until 8:45 PM. Closed Mondays and holidays.

Cost: $8.00 adults, $5.00 children and students; free on Sundays, 10 AM-1 PM.

Description: Children seem to enjoy large museums most when they can absorb the art in small bites. Instead of trying to see the whole museum, go with a specific exhibit in mind, such as the Indian Temple or the popular Arms & Armory display.

(*continued on next page*)

Budding young artists can understand a simple explanation of Impressionism, then check out the huge Impressionist paintings up close. Call to find out about new exhibits and the many popular events for children.

Time Needed: As long as a child's interest lasts.

Tours/Programs: Year-round family programs, films, lectures, tours, special performances, and children's activities. Family programs every Sunday.

Eating: Cafeteria and restaurant.

Phillips Mushroom Museum

909 East Baltimore Pike
Kennett Square, PA 19348
(610) 388-6082

Hours: Daily 10 AM-6 PM.

Cost: Free.

Description: Small exhibit and movie shows process of cultivating mushrooms. See real mushrooms growing.

Driving: Route 1 South from Philadelphia; watch for museum on your right after Chadds Ford.

Please Touch Museum

210 North 21st Street
Philadelphia, PA 19103
(215) 963-0667

Hours: September-June: daily 9 AM-4:30 PM; July-Labor Day: daily 9 AM-6 PM. Closed Thanksgiving, Christmas, and New Year's Day.

Cost: $6.95 per person, $5.00 seniors, under 1 free. Sunday, 9 AM-11 AM, pay as you wish.

Description: Here the emphasis is on children ages 7 and under. Changing exhibits tweak youngsters' curiosity while they play and learn. The Virginia Evans Theater schedules mime, puppetry, poetry, storytelling, and plays. Excellent shop with puzzles, games, books, and toys. No strollers allowed.

Time Needed: 1-2 hours.

Tours/Programs: Films, parent-child workshops, and outstanding special events throughout the year. "Traveling Trunks" bring Please Touch treasures to schools, scouts, even birthday parties.

Eating: Vending machines and benches in the Tortoise Lounge.

Reading Public Museum, Art Gallery and Planetarium

500 Museum Road
Reading, PA 19611
(610) 371-5850

Hours: Tuesday-Saturday, 11 AM-5 PM; Wednesday, 11 AM-8 PM; Sunday, 12 noon-5 PM. Closed Mondays and holidays. Planetarium shows: Sundays, 2 PM and 3 PM.

Cost: $4.00 adults, $2.00 children 4-17, under 4 free. Prices are subject to change with special exhibits. Planetarium: $3.00 adults, $2.00 children under 18.

Description: First-floor exhibits of birds, Native American crafts, prehistoric fossils, and minerals. Area on Eastern cultures, ancient civilizations, South Seas, and armor. Second floor has art gallery with changing exhibits.

Time Needed: 1-2 hours.

Tours/Programs: Plenty of tours and programs for children of all ages.

Eating: Playground across the street is possible for picnics.

Driving: I-76 (Schuylkill Expressway) West to Route 202 South to Route 422 North into Reading. Go through the center of the city, over Penn Street Bridge, then 3 more blocks to Fifth Avenue. Left on Fifth Avenue which turns into Museum Road. Museum is on the right.

Rodin Museum

26th Street and Ben Franklin Parkway
Philadelphia, PA 19101
(215) 763-8100 (Philadelphia Museum of Art)

Hours: Tuesday-Sunday, 10 AM-5 PM. Closed major holidays.

Cost: $3.00 donation requested.

Description: Anyone familiar with the French sculptor's beautiful work is delighted with Philadelphia's own collection, the largest outside Paris.

Rosenbach Museum and Library

2010 Delancey Place
Philadelphia, PA 19103
(215) 732-1600

Hours: Tuesday-Saturday, 11 AM-4 PM. Last tour 2:45 PM.

(*continued on next page*)

Cost: $5.00 adults, $3.00 students and seniors, $2.00 exhibition only.

Description: Maurice Sendak collection is readily recognized by children and explains book illustration from concept to finished product. As dealers and collectors, the Rosenbach brothers gathered drawings, paintings, and artifacts of literary figures and original manuscripts of writers from Chaucer to James Joyce. Combined with their antiques, the townhouse museum library and garden are a treat for anyone who appreciates first editions.

Ryerss Museum

7375 Central Avenue
Philadelphia, PA 19111
(215) 685-0599

Hours: Saturday and Sunday, 1 PM-4 PM, group tours by appointment. Library open Friday-Sunday, 10 AM-5 PM.

Cost: Free, donation appreciated.

Description: Family treasures like a stuffed alligator mixed with collections of armor, footwear and clothes from around the world, children's toys, and furniture.

Sanderson Museum

Route 100
Chadds Ford, PA 19317
(610) 388-6545

Hours: Saturday and Sunday, 1 PM-4:30 PM.

Cost: Donation requested.

Description: Christian Sanderson saved almost everything from his associations with the Wyeths and the Brandywine Valley. Also memorabilia from Revolutionary War, Civil War, WWI, and WWII.

Driving: I-95 South to Route 322 West to Route 1 South to Chadds Ford. Turn right onto Route 100 North. Museum is 100 yards ahead.

From 1790 to 1800, Philadelphia was the capital of the United States.

University Museum of Archaeology and Anthropology

University of Pennsylvania
33rd and Spruce Streets
Philadelphia, PA 19104
(215) 898-4000, or 222-7777 for schedule of events   ⅊ ⬆ 🚌 🎗 🛳

Hours: Tuesday-Saturday, 10 AM-4:30 PM; Sunday, 1 PM-5 PM. Closed Mondays, holidays, and summer Sundays.

Cost: $5.00 adults, $2.50 children and seniors, under 6 free.

Description: A visit to the Museum of Archaeology and Anthropology fits in well with almost any world culture children might be studying in school. Investigate mummies and cuneiform tablets, kachina dolls and tikis. The Pyramid Children's Shop is full of unusual, inexpensive treasures for active play.

Time Needed: 1-2 hours.

Tours/Programs: Excellent school programs arranged in advance. Foreign language tours available upon request.

Eating: Cafeteria-style restaurant.

Wagner Free Institute of Science

Montgomery Avenue and 17th Street
Philadelphia, PA 19121
(215) 763-6529   ⬆ 🚌 🎗 🚩

Hours: Tuesday-Friday, 9 AM-4 PM. Closed weekends and holidays.

Cost: Free.

Description: Collections of seashells, fossils, insects, minerals, birds, and mammals. Interesting nature programs scheduled daily for grade school children. Educational Loan Boxes available to teachers.

The Wagner Museum

900 Jacksonville Road
Ivyland, PA 18974
(215) 674-5000   ⬆

Hours: Monday-Saturday, 9:30 AM-4:30 PM.

Cost: Free.

(*continued on next page*)

Description: A small museum adjacent to the factory outlet takes visitors on a fascinating journey through the merchant's archives from 18th-century clipper ships to the present.

Directions: PA Turnpike to exit 27 (Willow Grove). Take Route 611 North about 4 1/2 miles to Route 132 (Street Road). Turn right on Route 132 about 4 miles to Jacksonville Road. Left on Jacksonville and watch for Wagner's Factory Outlet sign on left.

Watch and Clock Museum of the NAWCC

See Lancaster, page 170.

Wharton Esherick Museum

Box 595
Paoli, PA 19301
(610) 644-5822   ♿ 🍴 🚌 ⚓

Hours: Guided tours only. By reservation Saturdays, 10 AM-5 PM; Sundays, 1 PM-5 PM. Weekday group tours, 10 AM-4 PM.

Cost: $5.00 adults, $3.00 children under 12.

Description: Every inch of the sculptor's house and studio was handcrafted with enthusiasm and a sense of humor. Coat pegs carved to resemble friends, handcarved free-form stairs, walls, furniture, even light switches. Call ahead.

Driving: Curator gives directions when reservation is made.

Winterthur

See Glimpses of History, page 40.

Woodruff Indian Museum

See Bridgeton, page 151.

Philadelphia became the capital of Pennsylvania in 1790. In 1799, the state capital was moved to Lancaster and then to Harrisburg.

Ethnic Heritage Museums

Afro-American Historical and Cultural Museum

701 Arch Street
Philadelphia, PA 19106
(215) 574-0380

Hours: Tuesday-Saturday, 10 AM-5 PM; Sunday, 12 noon-5 PM. Closed holidays.

Cost: $6.00 adults, $4.00 children under 12, seniors, and students.

Description: Look for special exhibit just for children.

American Swedish Historical Museum

1900 Pattison Avenue
Philadelphia, PA 19145
(215) 389-1776

Hours: Tuesday-Friday, 10 AM-4 PM; Saturday and Sunday, 12 noon-4 PM. Closed Mondays and holidays.

Cost: $5.00 adults, $4.00 seniors and students 12-18, free for children under 12 accompanied by an adult.

Description: Galleries, special exhibits, and lots of fun activities.

Balch Institute for Ethnic Studies

18 South 7th Street
Philadelphia, PA 19106
(215) 925-8090

Hours: Monday-Saturday, 10 AM-4 PM.

Cost: $3.00 adults, $1.50 students and seniors.

Description: Good place to start to understand the immigration experience. Trace ancestry and drop marbles in the giant ethnic tally bank. Many good programs through Education Department.

German Society of Pennsylvania
611 Spring Garden Street
Philadelphia, PA 19123
(215) 627-4365

Hours: Library: Tuesday and Thursday, 10 AM-4 PM. Closed July and August.

Cost: Free.

Description: Founded in 1764, this is America's oldest German organization. Library has programs, exhibits, and special events.

Italian Market
See Working World, page 176.

Japanese House and Garden
See Fairmount Park, page 21.

Mennonite Heritage Center
See Lancaster, page 166.

National Museum of American Jewish History
Independence Mall East, 55 North Fifth Street
Philadelphia, PA 19106
(215) 923-3811

Hours: Monday-Thursday, 10 AM-5 PM; Friday, 10 AM-3 PM; Sunday, 12 noon-5 PM.

Cost: $3.00 adults, $2.00 students and seniors, under 5 free.

Description: Only museum in the country dedicated to the story of the Jewish role in the growth and development of America.

Polish American Cultural Center Museum
308 Walnut Street
Philadelphia, PA 19106
(215) 922-1700

Hours: Monday-Saturday, 10 AM-4 PM.

Cost: Free.

Description: Exhibits reflect the social and cultural heritage of Americans of Polish descent.

Quaker Information Center

1501 Cherry Street
Philadelphia, PA 19102
(215) 241-7024

Hours: Monday-Friday, 9 AM-5 PM.

Cost: Free.

Description: The place to go to learn more about the history of the Friends Society around the Delaware Valley.

Richard Allen Museum

Mother Bethel A.M.E. Church
419 South 6th Street
Philadelphia, PA 19147
(215) 925-0616

Hours: Tuesday-Saturday, 10 AM-3 PM.

Cost: Free.

Description: Tour the historic Mother Bethel Church, including the tombs of Richard and Sarah Allen.

Scottish Historic and Research Society of Delaware Valley

102 Saint Paul's Road
Ardmore, PA 19003
(610) 649-4144

Library open by reservation.
School programs available.

Historic Places of Worship

Philadelphia's earliest charter granted religious freedom to all, and immigrants came to these shores with high hopes. The places listed here encompass only a few of many diverse forms of worship. For more information, contact the Old Philadelphia Churches Historic Association (phone number changes annually; call Christ Church for current number).

Beth Shalom Synagogue

Old York Road and Foxcroft Road
Elkins Park, PA 19117
(215) 887-1342

Designed by Frank Lloyd Wright, one of America's greatest architects, the building is intended to represent Mount Sinai. A 30-minute tour further explains Wright's symbolism.

Bryn Athyn Swedenborgian Cathedral

Route 232 and Paper Mill Road
Bryn Athyn, PA 19009
(215) 947-0266

A Gothic Revival shrine with intricate details crafted by dedicated artisans. Make a reservation to visit the nearby Glencairn Museum while in Bryn Athyn.

Cathedral Basilica of Saints Peter and Paul

18th and Race Streets
Philadelphia, PA 19103
(215) 561-1313

Headquarters of the Roman Catholic Archdiocese of Philadelphia. Can seat 2000 at each Mass.

Cathedral of the Immaculate Conception
816 North Franklin Street
Philadelphia, PA 19123
(215) 922-2845

The largest Ukrainian Catholic cathedral in the world. Notice its famous golden dome.

Christ Church
2nd and Market Streets
Philadelphia, PA 19106
(215) 922-1695

Considered the birthplace of the Protestant Episcopal Church in the United States. Seven signers of the Declaration of Independence worshipped here, each with his own pew in which he sat with his family. Look for some of their names on the pews. Ben Franklin and other colonial heroes are buried in the churchyard at 5th and Arch.

Ephrata Cloister
See Lancaster, page 164.

Mennonite Meeting House
6119 Germantown Avenue
Philadelphia, PA 19144
(215) 843-0943

Meeting place for the first Mennonite congregation in the colonies, restored to look as it did in the late 1700's, including the well in the basement.

Mikveh Israel Synagogue
44 North 4th Street
Philadelphia, PA 19106
(215) 922-5446

The oldest synagogue in Philadelphia, second oldest in the country. Tour includes synagogue and adjacent National Museum of American Jewish History.

Mother Bethel A.M.E. Church

419 Richard Allen Avenue
Philadelphia, PA 19147
(215) 925-0616

First African Methodist Episcopal church. Tour explains the history of Black ownership and shows the beautiful stained glass windows. See also Richard Allen Museum, page 76.

Old First Reformed Church

4th and Race Streets
Philadelphia, PA 19106
(215) 922-4566

German refugees established this church in 1727. Don't miss the nativity scene in the courtyard with live animals during the last two weeks in December.

Old Pine Street Presbyterian Church

Fourth and Pine Streets
Philadelphia, PA 19106
(215) 925-8051

The one remaining colonial Presbyterian church in Philadelphia. When the British occupied the city during the Revolution, it was used as a hospital and then as a stable for the cavalry.

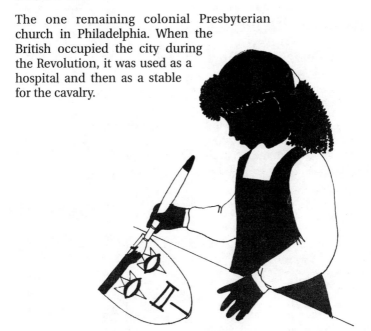

Old Saint Joseph's Church

Willings Alley, near 4th and Walnut Streets
Philadelphia, PA 19106
(215) 923-1733

Oldest Roman Catholic church in Philadelphia. Founded in 1732, it was the only church in the colonies where public celebration of the Mass was permitted by law.

Old Swedes Church

606 Church Street
Wilmington, DE 19801
(302) 652-5629

Oldest church in the United States—originally Lutheran, then Protestant Episcopal. An outstanding brochure explains it all.

Our Lady of Czestochowa

Ferry Road
Doylestown, PA 18901
(215) 345-0600

This American counterpart of a 12th-century shrine in Poland stands in a lovely 240-acre setting. Stained glass windows are among the largest in the world.

Saint Peter's Episcopal Church

313 Pine Street
Philadelphia, PA 19106
(215) 925-5968

A beautiful brick church with box pews, built in 1761. George and Martha Washington worshipped here. Graveyard has many distinguished residents, including seven Indian chiefs.

Nature

Whether you're looking for elephants at a zoo, birds of prey at Hawk Mountain, or the bugs and slugs of everyday life, you'll find them here.

Nature outings don't have to be a big deal. Take just half an hour to walk through a garden or along a woodland path in a nature center. Watch the butterflies and turn over rocks to see who lives there.

If you have the time and the inclination, explore a cave or feed animals on a farm. Try the insectarium. Older children are fascinated with planetariums and observatories.

Look for the natural history and science museums in the preceding chapter under "Collections."

The state beverage of Pennsylvania is milk.

Animal Rehabilitation Centers

Marine Mammal Stranding Center
3625 Brigantine Boulevard
P.O. Box 773
Brigantine, NJ 08203
(609) 266-0538   &. ♠

Hours: Labor Day-Memorial Day: Saturday-Sunday, 12 noon-4 PM; Memorial Day-Labor Day: daily 11 AM-5 PM.

Cost: $1.00 donation per person is suggested.

Description: A small, out-of-the-way treasure, the stranding center rescues and rehabilitates many marine mammals each year. Visitors can walk through the museum with its touch tanks and try to identify the animal casts hanging all around. You also may hear about some mammals in residence and the work the center is doing to set them free.

Driving: Follow the Atlantic City Expressway into Atlantic City. Follow signs for Trump Castle Casino and State Marina. Take Brigantine Bridge (between Harrah's and Trump Castle) into Brigantine. Center is on Brigantine Boulevard on left, 2 miles from bridge.

Ryerss' Farm for Aged Equines
Ridge Road (Route 23), R.D. 2
Pottstown, PA 19464
(610) 469-0533   &. 🚐

Hours: Daily 10 AM-4 PM. Call first.

Cost: Donations appreciated.

Description: A retirement home for horses. If you call and make reservations, the staff will take your family or school group on a tour of the facilities, including two barns and crop fields.

Driving: PA Turnpike west to exit 23 (Downingtown). Take Route 100 North to Route 23. Go west on Route 23 for 2 1/2 miles. Watch for fence on your right.

Wetlands Institute

1075 Stone Harbor Boulevard
Stone Harbor, NJ 08247
(609) 368-1211

Hours: May-October: Monday-Saturday, 9:30 AM-4:30 PM; Sunday, 10 AM-4 PM; October-May: Tuesday-Saturday, 9:30 AM-4:30 PM.

Cost: $5.00 adults, $2.00 children 3-12, under 3 free.

Description: Coastal wetlands play an important part in our ecosystem, and here's the place to learn. "Wetlandia" is a children's discovery room with games and exhibits; another educational area features saltwater aquaria and marsh-related exhibits. Outside, explore a salt marsh trail, a marsh boardwalk, gardens filled with birds and butterflies, and an observation tower. In the summer, be sure to come inside to watch a live taping of an osprey nest.

Eating: Outdoor picnic tables.

Directions: Walt Whitman Bridge to Route 42 South to the Atlantic City Expressway, east to the Garden State Parkway, south to exit 10. Turn left at light. Go 2 1/2 miles. Institute is on right.

Aquarium

New Jersey State Aquarium & Children's Garden

1 Riverside Drive
Camden, NJ 08105-1060
(609) 365-3300   ⅙ ⚲ 🚎 ♨ 🚢 🚩
www.njaquarium.org

> *(Strollers permitted only during off-peak times.*
> *Backpacks are available, free of charge.)*

Hours: September-March: 10 AM-5 PM; March-September: 9:30 AM-5:30 PM. Closed Thanksgiving, Christmas, and New Year's Day.

Cost: $11.95 adults, $10.45 seniors and students, $8.95 children 3-11, under 3 free.

Description: An exciting place to visit with interactive exhibits both inside and out. The Ocean Base Atlantic exhibit and touch tanks, where you can actually stroke the small sharks and rays swimming by, keep all ages busy. Play in the Children's Garden and wander through recreations of "Alice in Wonderland," "The Three Little Pigs," "Jack and the Beanstalk," and more. The Dinosaur Garden and Treehouse are also worth the climb.

Time Needed: 2 hours to half a day.

Tours/Programs: Many exciting programs for all ages throughout the year.

Eating: Riverview Cafe inside or on outdoor deck overlooking Delaware River.

Directions: Take Benjamin Franklin Bridge across to Camden. After going through toll in Camden, stay to the right, following signs for I-676 and the Mickle Boulevard exit. Or take the RiverLink Ferry from Penn's Landing. Ferry leaves Walnut Street at Penn's Landing on the hour (10 AM-5 PM) and from the Aquarium every hour on the half hour (10:30 AM-5:30 PM). Round-trip fare is $5.00 per person for adults, $3.00 for children, and $4.00 for seniors. Group rates available. For more RiverLink Ferry information, call 215-925-5465.

Caves

(Be sure to bring a sweater for these tours as the temperature in the caves and caverns is a constant 52°.)

Crystal Cave

R.D. 3
Kutztown, PA 19530
(610) 683-6765
www.crystalcavepa.com

Hours: March-April: daily 9 AM-5 PM; May: Monday-Friday 9 AM-5 PM; Saturday, Sunday, and holidays, 9 AM-6 PM; Memorial Day-Labor Day: Monday-Friday, 9 AM-6 PM; Saturday-Sunday, 9 AM-7 PM; Labor Day-November: daily 9 AM-5 PM.

Cost: $8.00 adults, $4.75 children 4-11, under 4 free.

Description: Visit the cave with the ballroom and amazing underground formations, then go outside and enjoy 125 acres of nature trails, picnic area, playground, and various shops.

Time Needed: 1 to 2 hours. Must go on tour through cave, approximately 45 minutes, including introductory video presentation.

Tours/Programs: 45-minute tours run continually throughout the day. Special Halloween night tours on the last three weekends of October.

Driving: I-76 West to Route 476 North to PA Turnpike. Take the Northeast Extension (Route 9N) to exit 33—Lehigh Valley. Follow Route 22 West to exit 11, then Route 143 for 7 miles toward Lenhartsville.

Lost River Caverns

Hellertown, PA 18055
(610) 838-8767
www.lostcave.com

Hours: Memorial Day-Labor Day: 9 AM-6 PM; Labor Day-Memorial Day: 9 AM-5 PM. Closed Thanksgiving, Christmas, and New Year's Day.

Cost: $8.00 adults, $4.00 children 3-12, under 3 free.

Description: The half-hour tour of these caverns will take you through five underground chambers to look at stalactites, stalagmites, helectites, drip stones, flow stones, and a natural stream.

Eating: Picnic area.

Driving: Northeast Extension of the PA Turnpike to exit 33 (Lehigh Valley). Follow Route 22 East to Route 309 South to I-78 East. Take exit 21 (Bethlehem/Hellertown). Turn left at light onto Route 412 South. At third light, turn left onto Penn Street. Caverns are half a mile on the right.

Farms

Amish Farm and House
See Lancaster, page 161.

Colonial Pennsylvania Plantation
See Villages and Homesteads, page 43.

Fox Chase Farm
Pine Road at Pennypack Creek
P.O. Box 21601
Philadelphia, PA 19131
(215) 728-7900 or call Pennypack Environmental Center
at (215) 685-0470.

Hours: Summer Sundays, 1 PM-4 PM, and many other days for special events and school groups. Call ahead for schedules and reservations.

Cost: Free.

Description: 45-minute guided tour of 112-acre working farm—the last one in Philadelphia. Dairy cows, cattle, sheep, pigs, a horse, cornfields, apple orchard, and more. Each Sunday in summer features a special craft presentation ranging from ice cream or butter churning, beekeeping, and woodworking, to chick hatching and vegetable printing. Other special events include maple sugar tapping, sheepshearing, and family farm day.

Tours/Programs: Many programs for school groups who experience hands-on activities.

Eating: Picnic tables; lemonade and cookies sold.

Freddy Hill Farms
1440 Sumneytown Pike
Lansdale, PA 19446
(215) 855-1205

Hours: Farm and ice cream parlor: 9 AM-9 PM; Cow milking: 4 PM-6 PM; Miniature golf, driving range, and batting cages: vary by season, call for hours.

(*continued on next page*)

Cost: Petting zoo and farm: free. Miniature golf, driving range, and batting cages: Saturday-Sunday, $5.00 per person, $3.00 children under 5; Monday-Friday, $4.00 per person, $2.50 children under 5.

Description: Small petting zoo with farm animals including goats, sheep, pigs, a horse, and calves. There is also an area where you can see buffalo, elk, deer, a donkey, emus, alpacas, and pheasants. Freddy's Fall Fest each weekend in October highlights the year with pony rides, hay rides, face painting, and more. They even won the award for "Philly's Best Ice Cream" in 1999!

Time Needed: 1 hour.

Eating: Picnic area.

Driving: I-76 (Schuylkill Expressway) West to Route 202 South, to Route 422 North, to Route 363 North (Valley Forge Road). Continue about 10 1/2 miles. Turn left onto Sumneytown Pike. Farm is about half a mile on left.

Howell Living History Farm

Box 187, R.R. 2, Hunter Road
Titusville, NJ 08560
(609) 737-3299

Hours: Last week of January to the first week of December: Tuesday-Saturday, 10 AM-4 PM; Sunday, 12 noon-4 PM. Closed the rest of December and January. The last three Saturdays in July: open 5 PM-8 PM for hayrides.

Cost: Farm: free (donations appreciated). Corn maze: $6.50 adults, $4.50 children.

Description: Join the farming life. Help plant, pick, or grind corn depending on the season. See some animals, crops, and 19th-century implements. Hayrides and children's craft and music programs are offered throughout the year. Come try to find your way through the corn maze in August, September, and October.

Time Needed: 1 hour.

Tours/Programs: Living history programs open to the public offer year-round activities showing life as it was in the early 1900's. Call ahead and time your visit to coincide with craft days or organized activities.

Eating: Picnic area.

Driving: I-95 North into New Jersey. Take first New Jersey exit, follow Route 29 North for 8 miles toward Lambertville. Right on Valley Road for 1 1/2 miles, entrance on left.

Merrymead Farm

2222 Valley Forge Road (Route 363)
Lansdale, PA 19446
(610) 584-4410   ♿ 🚌

Hours: Summer months: Monday-Friday, 6:30 AM-10 PM; Saturday, 8 AM-10 PM; Sunday, 11 AM-10 PM. Winter months: Monday-Friday, 6:30 AM-9 PM; Saturday, 8 AM-9 PM; Sunday, 12 noon-8 PM.

Cost: Free, but there is a charge for group tours and hayrides.

Description: Busy, family-owned and operated farm with constant supply of new baby animals being born. Touch the sheep, donkey, goat, cows, and calves. Sheepshearing in spring, live nativity in winter. Cows milked 3:30 PM-6 PM.

Time Needed: 1 hour.

Eating: Assorted foods available, including delicious homemade ice cream served in a pretzel cone.

Driving: I-76 (Schuylkill Expressway) West to Route 202 South, to Route 422 North, to Route 363 North (Valley Forge Road). Go about 10 miles, cross Skippack Pike (Route 73). Farm on right.

Norview Farm

670 N. Henderson Road
King of Prussia, PA 19406
(610) 265-2933   ♿ 🚌

Hours: Daily 8 AM-9 PM.

Cost: Free.

Description: Not far from the Court and the Mall at King of Prussia, Norview is small, easy and fun to visit. Feed the livestock, see farm babies in spring, buy fresh dairy milk and ice cream.

Driving: Schuylkill Expressway (I-76) west to Route 202 North. After the Malls, watch for Henderson Road on the left. Go left on N. Henderson Road, past one light, then watch for Norview's giant rooster on the right.

> **Before the Dutch settlers arrived, the Lenni-Lenape Indians inhabited the land now called Pennsylvania, New Jersey, and Delaware.**

Springton Manor Farm

Springton Road, Box 117
Glenmoore, PA 19343
(610) 942-2450

Hours: Park: dawn to dusk; office: daily 7 AM-3:30 PM.

Cost: Free.

Description: This 400-acre working farm dates back to William Penn. Crops, sheep, pigs, chickens, and more around the barn. Watch for paved path for wheelchairs and strollers, wander through meadow and woods, then out to dock built for wheelchair fishing only. Exciting special events throughout the year.

Driving: PA Turnpike west to exit 22 (Morgantown). Go south on Route 100, west on Route 30, north on Route 322 through Guthriesville to Little Washington. Go right onto Springton Road. Farm is 2 1/2 miles ahead.

Upper Schuylkill Valley Park and Wildlife Center

Route 113
Royersford, PA 19468
(610) 948-5170

Hours: Outdoors and indoors: 8 AM-dusk.

Cost: Free.

Description: Good, small, county-operated farm located on 125 acres. Wide variety of local wildlife, including black bears, bobcats, foxes, raccoons, owls, chickens, and a pair of wolves.

Eating: Picnic area by river.

Driving: I-76 (Schuylkill Expressway) West to Route 202 South, to Route 422 West. Take Route 422 West from King of Prussia to Oaks exit. Go left under Route 422, take first right onto Black Rock Road. Follow Black Rock Road approximately 4 miles. Go left onto Route 113. Farm with small sign is across from Montgomery County Geriatric and Rehabilitation Center.

Wentz Farmstead

See Villages and Homesteads, page 47.

Gardens and Arboretums

Awbury Arboretum
See Germantown, page 152.

Bartram's House and Gardens
54th Street and Lindbergh Boulevard
Philadelphia, PA 19143
(215) 729-5281

Hours: Grounds: daily, 10 AM-5 PM. House: March-December, Tuesday-Sunday, 12 noon-4 PM; January-February, by appointment only.

Cost: $3.00 adults, $2.75 seniors, $2.00 children 6-12.

Description: The Bartrams (father and two sons) collected New World seeds as early as 1730, from as far away as Canada and Florida. They planted them here, then distributed seeds and plants to others. Gardens are full of pungent herbs; path along river is great for exploring. Watch for archaeological work in progress. Note the root cellar and ice pit. New exhibits include a wetland and aquatic plant garden as well as a native plant exhibit based on the 1783 Bartram catalogue.

Tours/Programs: Special programs, by appointment only, include segments on colonial life, a colonial craft project and, in good weather, an outdoor botany lesson.

Bowman's Hill Wildflower Preserve
1635 River Road
New Hope, PA 18938
(215) 862-2924

Hours: Daily 8:30 AM-sunset. Tours: March-October, 2 PM. Office: Daily 9 AM-5 PM.

Cost: Free. Tours, $3.00 adults, $5.00 family.

Description: Located in Washington Crossing Historic Park (see page 39), this wildflower preserve includes trails that wind through 100 beautiful acres. Children are welcome for nature movies on Sunday afternoons in winter.

Eating: Picnic area.

Driving: Take I-95 North to New Hope/Yardley exit; go left off the ramp onto Taylorsville Road toward New Hope. Go 3 miles to a light, go right onto Route 532, then left onto Route 32 (River Road). Visitors Center is on your right.

George Read II House and Garden
See Glimpses of History, page 29.

Hershey Gardens
See Hershey, page 158.

Horticulture Center
See Fairmount Park, page 21.

Jenkins Arboretum
631 Berwyn-Baptist Road
Devon, PA 19333
(610) 647-8870

Hours: Daily, dawn to dusk.

Cost: Free.

Description: Located on a hillside, where children love to run up and down steep paths leading to the pond full of ducks and geese. Good anytime for a short outing in the woods.

Driving: I-76 (Schuylkill Expressway) West to Route 202 South, to Devon exit. Take left onto Devon State Road and follow it up the hill over the bridge, then bear right. Watch for sign ahead on right.

Longwood Gardens
Route 1, Box 501
Kennett Square, PA 19348-0501
(610) 388-6741 or (800) 737-5500

Hours: November-March: daily 9 AM-5 PM; April-October: daily 9 AM-6 PM. Indoors, daily 10 AM-5 PM.

Cost: $12.00 adults (Tuesdays: $8:00 adults); $6.00 ages 6-15; under 6 free.

Description: Giant real banana trees, massive water lily pads capable of holding a person, and plants trained as topiary animals are just a few of the many horticultural wonders that appeal to children. Elaborate Christmas displays sparkle with imagination. Children's Garden introduces youngsters to the wonders of bright flowers and plants grown as mazes and tunnels—it also lets them play with small fountains without getting too wet.

Time Needed: 2-3 hours.

(*continued on next page*)

Tours/Programs: Diverse summer programs, including "Ice Cream Concerts" and the spectacular fireworks-music-fountain symphonies are all special treats. Request schedules and reservations early. Popular activities fill up quickly, especially fireworks. On summer weekends, visit the Kids' Corner which features garden programs for children.

Eating: Full-service restaurant, cafeteria, picnic area.

Driving: I-95 South to Route 322 West, to Route 1 South. In about 8 miles, watch for signs for Longwood Gardens, located approximately 4 miles south of Chadds Ford.

Morris Arboretum of the University of Pennsylvania

100 Northwestern Avenue
Philadelphia, PA 19118
(215) 247-5777, or 242-3399

Hours: All year: Monday-Friday, 10 AM-4 PM; April-October: Saturday-Sunday, 10 AM-5 PM; November-March: Saturday-Sunday, 10 AM-4 PM. Closed Thanksgiving, Christmas, and New Year's Day. Guided tours: Saturday-Sunday, 2 PM.

Cost: $6.00 adults, $4.00 students, children under 6 free. Group rates available.

Description: Living museum of plants. Weeping beech tree is the favorite of children who want to hide from their friends. Wide variety of plants in the rose garden, azalea meadow, fern house, and other specialized growing areas. Summer features include a garden railway display with model trains and historic replicas of Philadelphia buildings. Look for the waterfall and a trestle bridge made of twigs. Great fun for all ages.

Time Needed: 1 hour.

Tours/Programs: Age-appropriate games for school groups cover the subjects of fall color, plant exploring, the importance of bark, and many others.

Driving: Schuylkill Expressway (I-76) to Lincoln Drive exit. Follow Drive to end, go right on Allen's Lane, go left onto Germantown Avenue. Follow Germantown Avenue for 4 miles through Chestnut Hill. Turn right at Northwestern Avenue, then right into Arboretum gate.

Pennsbury Manor

See Glimpses of History, page 36.

Pennsylvania Hospital Physic Garden

8th and Pine Streets
Philadelphia, PA 19107
(215) 829-7352 &

Hours: Dawn to dusk.

Cost: Free.

Description: A special city retreat. Ben Franklin's hospital staff requested a physic garden where they could grow medicinal herbs. This garden was created for the Bicentennial, using the original plans. Pennsylvania Hospital's public relations office offers a good brochure describing the plants and their uses. Easy lesson for children on the vital link between plants and humans. The shaded "woodland" walk is cooling on a hot summer day.

Time Needed: 30 minutes.

Scott Arboretum of Swarthmore College

500 College Avenue
Swarthmore, PA 19081
(610) 328-8025 & 🚐 🎭

Hours: Daily, dawn to dusk, all year.

Cost: Free.

Description: A sculpture area resembling Stonehenge in the meadow along Crum Creek delights youngsters familiar with the English original. Tours include greenhouses and an avenue of stately white oaks, some 100 years old. Over 5000 different kinds of plants are growing on the grounds. Children love the Terry Shane Teaching Garden and the fish pond behind the Arboretum headquarters. Woodland paths and newly restored trails appeal to all ages.

Eating: Snack bar in Clothier Hall, open during school year.

Driving: I-76 (Schuylkill Expressway) West to Route 320. Follow 320 South 14 1/2 miles to College Avenue. Turn right on College Avenue and go one block to Arboretum office.

Taylor Memorial Arboretum

10 Ridley Drive
Wallingford, PA 19086
(610) 876-2649

Hours: Daily 9 AM-4 PM. Closed major holidays.

Cost: Free.

Description: This conservation project features a plant sanctuary with an old quarry site known as Anne's Grotto, a waterfall, pond, woodland and meadow habitats.

Driving: From I-95, take Route 320 North. About half a mile before intersection of Routes 320 and 252, go west on Chestnut Parkway. Go half a mile to Ridley Drive on left, then follow signs for the Arboretum.

Tyler Arboretum

515 Painter Road
P.O. Box 216
Lima, PA 19037
(610) 566-5431

Hours: Grounds: daily 8 AM-dusk. Tours of historic buildings: April-June and September-October: Sunday, 1 PM-4 PM.

Cost: $5.00 adults, $3.00 children, under 3 free.

Description: More than 650 acres adjoin the 2600 acres of Ridley Creek State Park and visitors get a true feeling of the natural countryside. Well-marked trails and the Stockford Family Meadow Maze appeal to energetic children any time of the year. Pets allowed if on leashes. Specialty gardens include paintings that encourage butterflies, bird habitats, herbs, and fragrances. Large numbers of bluebirds and their houses.

Tours/Programs: Nature programs and natural crafts for ages 4 and over.

Eating: No food allowed. Snacks available in bookstore.

Driving: Schuylkill Expressway (I-76) to Route 476 South to exit 3. Follow Route 1 South. Stay in right lane, go right on Route 352 North, then right on Barren Road. Go 1 mile to four-way stop, left on Painter Road. Watch for arboretum signs 1 mile ahead on right.

Winterthur

See Glimpses of History, page 40.

Insectarium

The Insectarium

Steve's Bug Off Exterminating Co.
8046 Frankford Avenue
Philadelphia, PA 19136
(215) 335-9500

Hours: Monday-Saturday, 10 AM-4 PM. Closed major holidays.

Cost: $4.00 per person, 2 and under free.

Description: They're all here—insects, arachnids (spiders), crustaceans, chilopoda (centipedes), and diplopoda (millipedes). Live and mounted specimens, including cockroach kitchen, working beehive, live termite tunnel, many tarantulas, camouflage insects, and numerous butterflies with mirror images. Great interactive exhibits. Amazing murals. Stand on scale and find out how many ladybugs, fruitflies, or lightning bugs you weigh!

Tours/Programs: Tours and programs available for school groups. Saturday activities for families based on monthly themes. Join Kids Bug Club, and Insectarium's Traveling Zoo will visit your group.

Nature Centers

Airdrie Forest Preserve

Fennerton Road
Paoli, PA 19301
(610) 647-5380 (answers Open Land Conservancy)

Hours: Dawn to dusk.

Cost: Free.

Description: 75 woodland acres with a stream offer opportunities for walks in the woods and nature appreciation. Trails do not cover the whole preserve but are just the right length for children.

Driving: Schuylkill Expressway (I-76) to Route 476 South to St. David's/Villanova exit. Turn left and follow Route 30 West to Paoli. At center of Paoli, immediately after the Paoli train station, go right on North Valley Road, then right on Central Avenue, then left on Fennerton. Go to the end of the street. Watch carefully for small sign on right.

Andorra Natural Area

See Fairmount Park, page 20.

Ashland Nature Center of the Delaware Nature Society

Brackenville and Barley Mill Roads
Hockessin, DE 19707
(302) 239-2334
www.delawarenaturesociety.org

Hours: Monday-Friday, 8:30 AM-4:30 PM; Saturday, 9 AM-3 PM; Sunday, 1 PM-4 PM. Closed holidays.

Cost: Donations for trail use.

Description: Indoor exhibits feature a children's corner. Outside, visit the native plant demonstration garden and 4 miles of self-guided trails. From mid-June to September, the butterfly house offers a close-up view of these beautiful insects.

Eating: Picnic tables.

(continued on next page)

Driving: I-95 South to Delaware Avenue exit (Route 52 North). Follow Route 52 North through Greenville, then go left onto Route 82 North. After 4 miles, Route 82 takes a sharp left. After the railroad tracks, go left on an unmarked road, through the covered bridge, and watch for Nature Center on right.

Tours/Programs: Special programs include the Harvest Moon Festival in October, the Native Plant Sale in May, plus other events throughout the year.

Briar Bush Nature Center

Edge Hill Road
Abington, PA 19001
(215) 887-6603

Hours: Trails open until dusk. Pond, Observatory, and Museum: Monday-Saturday, 9 AM-5 PM; Sunday, 1 PM-5 PM.

Cost: Free. Discovery Den: $1.00 per child.

Description: Twelve acres with paths that wind around ponds and a well-marked bird observatory. Inside, Discovery Den for preschoolers and lots of hands-on material for all ages: hold a mouse skull next to a cow's skull, feel different animal "coverings."

Tours/Programs: Many good programs. Advance reservations required.

Eating: Benches and picnic tables outside.

Driving: PA Turnpike to exit 27 (Willow Grove). Go south on Route 611 for about 3 miles and turn right onto Edge Hill Road. Briar Bush is half a mile on right.

> **Pennsylvania has more than 8 million acres of "Green Space" (preserved land). At any point within the state you are within 25 miles from a state park.**

> **The state insect of Pennsylvania is the lightning bug. It is one of the few insects children go out of their way to catch!**

Camden County Environmental Studies Center
Park Drive and Estaugh Avenue
Berlin, NJ 08009
(856) 767-7275 or (856) 768-1598　　　　　　 ♿ ⇑ 🚌

Hours: By appointment only.

Cost: Free for Camden County residents; small fee for others.

Description: Small nature center with 5 miles of walking trails. Emphasis on group programs. Outstanding reference materials.

Eating: Picnic areas in park.

Driving: Ben Franklin Bridge to New Jersey, follow Route 30 for approximately 15 miles into Berlin. In the middle of the business district, go right onto Broad Avenue and continue to the end. Entrance is straight ahead.

Churchville Nature Center
501 Churchville Lane
Churchville, PA 18966
(215) 357-4005　　　　　　 ♿ 🚌

Hours: Grounds: daily, dawn to dusk; Nature Center: Tuesday-Sunday, 10 AM-5 PM. Closed Mondays and holidays.

Cost: Free.

Description: Trail map available in Nature Center to direct you along fun trails winding around beehives, ponds, quarry pits, reservoir, and marsh. Outdoor classrooms revel in the wonders of nature. Lots of ducks and other wildlife.

Eating: Picnic tables.

Driving: PA Turnpike to exit 27 (Willow Grove). Follow Route 611 North to Street Road (Route 132). Turn right onto Route 132 East, then left onto Route 232 North. At first light, turn right onto Bristol Road. At first light, turn left onto Churchville Lane. Cross lake, Nature Center on left.

Tours/Programs: Recorded phone message details dates. Special program offered to school groups about the Lenape Indians.

> The state tree of New Jersey is the red oak and the state flower is the purple violet.

Cool Valley Preserve

Cool Valley Road
Paoli, PA 19301
(610) 647-5380 (answers Open Land Conservancy)

Hours: Dawn to dusk.

Cost: Free.

Description: Peaceful outing with walk along nature trails and Valley Creek. Plenty of open fields and views.

Driving: Schuylkill Expressway (I-76) to Route 476 South to St. David's/Villanova exit. Turn left at light and go west on Route 30 to Paoli. In the center of Paoli, immediately after train station, go right on North Valley Road, left on Swedesford Road, then right on Shadow Oak Drive. Turn right on Cool Valley Road; entrance is on your right. Watch carefully for sign.

Four Mills Nature Reserve (Wissahickon Valley Watershed)

12 Morris Road
Ambler, PA 19002
(215) 646-8866

Hours: Monday-Friday, 9 AM-5 PM. Closed Saturdays, Sundays, and major holidays.

Cost: Free.

Description: Good small nature center in old barn with many fun activities, like matching animals with their tracks and comparing the sizes of birds' nests. Learn about food chains and how birds' beaks adapt to the type of food they eat.

Programs: Many throughout the year.

Driving: PA Turnpike to exit 26 (Fort Washington). Go straight after toll booths, bearing right onto Pennsylvania Avenue (not marked). At dead end, turn left onto Bethlehem Pike (Route 309). Just after train station and small bridge, take a right at restaurant onto Morris Road. Nature Center is 1 mile ahead on the right.

Pennsylvania covers 29 million acres and is 1/12th the size of Alaska and 38 times larger than Rhode Island.

George Lorimer Nature Preserve

North Valley Road
Paoli, PA 19301
(610) 647-5380 (answers Open Land Conservancy)

Hours: Dawn to dusk.

Cost: Free.

Description: Trails through the woods and around the pond plus open fields offer a great walk any time of year.

Driving: Schuylkill Expressway (I-76) to Route 476 South to St. David's/Villanova exit. Turn left at light and follow Route 30 West to Paoli. In the center of Paoli, immediately after Paoli train station, go right on North Valley Road, then right on Swedesford Road, then left onto North Valley again. Entrance is on the right. Watch carefully for sign.

Great Valley Nature Center

P.O. Box 82, Route 29 and Hollow Road
Devault, PA 19432
(610) 935-9777

Hours: Monday-Saturday, 9 AM-5 PM; Sunday, 12 noon-5 PM. Closed major holidays.

Cost: Donations appreciated.

Description: 10 1/2 acres of nature trails to explore outside with a wide variety of land and water animal habitats. Good indoor exhibit room and new outdoor raptor center which features two bald eagles.

Tours/Programs: Fun exploration programs all year-round for youngsters and their families. Children grades 7-12 may volunteer to be summer nature camp aides for the junior group.

Eating: Picnics permitted.

Driving: I-76 (Schuylkill Expressway) West to Route 202 South. Take Route 29 exit, go right (29 North) to Hollow Road. Turn left on Hollow Road, watch for small parking lot on right. Park there, then walk over bridge and up hill to Nature Center.

King of Prussia was named for a tavern, King of Prussia Inn, established in the area in 1709 by a native of Prussia. The tavern was named for Frederick I, the Brandenburg Prince.

Gwynedd Wildlife Preserve

640 Swedesford Road
Ambler, PA 19002
(215) 699-6751

Hours: Open dawn to dusk, call for parking availability.

Cost: Free.

Description: The Natural Lands Trust, Inc. is developing this property as a wildlife preserve. Features 230 acres, 4 miles of trails, woodland paths, an open meadow, and two ponds. Programs for children available by appointment.

Driving: PA Turnpike to exit 26 (Fort Washington). Take Route 309 North to Springhouse exit. At bottom of ramp, turn left onto Springhouse-Norristown Road. Go 3 miles and watch for Wm. Penn Inn on the left. Then left at Swedesford Road and look for number 640 and the Gwynedd sign on the right.

Hawk Mountain Sanctuary

Route 2, Box 191
Kempton, PA 19529
(610) 756-6961   ♿ (*Visitors Center*)

Hours: Trails open dawn to dusk. Visitors Center, daily 9 AM-5 PM; September-November, daily 8 AM-5 PM. Closed Christmas.

Cost: Visitors Center free; hiking trails $4.00 adults, $3.00 seniors, $2.00 children 6-12, under 6 free. Fall weekends: $6.00 adults, $4.00 seniors, $3.00 children.

Description: A 2400-acre refuge for birds of prey with numerous lookout spots. From mid-August through mid-December, view thousands of hawks, eagles, and falcons as they migrate through the area. You might also see migrating hummingbirds, warblers, swifts, and swallows in the fall. Be sure to stop at the Visitors Center for a brochure before starting out.

Eating: Picnics permitted at lookout sites. Light snacks available at the sanctuary.

Driving: PA Turnpike to the Northeast Extension to exit 33 (Lehigh Valley). Go west on Route 22, north on Route 61, north on Route 895, and east on Route 737. Sanctuary is 6 miles short of Kempton. (Parking lots fill quickly on October weekends, so arrive early!)

John Heinz National Wildlife Refuge at Tinicum

U.S. Fish and Wildlife Service
86th Street and Lindbergh Boulevard
Philadelphia, PA 19153
(215) 365-3118   ♿ 🚌

Hours: Outdoors: daily 8 AM-sunset. Visitors Center: daily 8:30 AM-4 PM.

Cost: Free.

Description: Largest tidal wetland in Pennsylvania. Trails open all year for walking and good bird watching; over 280 species of birds have been sighted here. New education center is worth exploring.

Eating: Picnics allowed along trails.

Mill Grove, Audubon Wildlife Sanctuary

P.O. Box 473
Audubon, PA 19407
(610) 666-5593   🔴 🚌

Hours: Grounds: daily 7 AM-dusk; Museum: Tuesday-Saturday, 10 AM-4 PM; Sunday, 1-4 PM. Closed Mondays, Thanksgiving, Christmas, and New Year's Day.

Cost: Free.

Description: First (and only remaining) American home of artist/naturalist John James Audubon. Giant murals on the mansion's walls depict Audubon's adventures and many bird scenes. Restored studio and taxidermy room. Well-marked trails are short enough for young children to complete. Take along crayons and paper so young artists can imitate Audubon.

Programs: Folder available listing 174 species of birds sighted.

Eating: Picnicking allowed.

Driving: I-76 (Schuylkill Expressway) West to Route 202 South to Route 422 West to Audubon exit (Route 363). Bear right along exit ramp, then left onto Audubon Road. Mill Grove is straight ahead at dead end.

Nolde Forest Environmental Education Center

R.D. 1, Box 392
Reading, PA 19607
(610) 796-3699

Hours: Outdoors: dawn to dusk. Office and mansion: Monday-Friday, 8 AM-4 PM.

Cost: Free.

Description: Truly for nature appreciation. Hiking OK, but no swimming, eating, or camping. Stop by the office and pick up a topographical leaflet, then enjoy 600 acres of protected land. A few paved trails for wheelchairs and strollers.

Tours/Programs: Good school group programs. Call ahead.

Driving: PA Turnpike to Morgantown exit 22. Take Morgantown Road onto Route 625 for 2 miles. Entrance is after second sign saying Nolde Forest. Watch carefully, entrance is obscure.

PAWS Farm Nature Center

(Preservation and Wildlife Sanctuary)
Hainesport-Mount Laurel Road
Mount Laurel, NJ 08054
(609) 778-8795

Hours: Wednesday-Sunday, 10 AM-4 PM.

Cost: $3.00 adults, $2.00 children.

Description: Visit over 70 animals along the nature trail, in the barnyard, and even in the historic house. Inside the nature center, try the hands-on activities for children including the pretend vet's office, the "moo-trition" market with displays on cow milking and dairy products, and the new Land, Sea and Forest area. Also on the historic property are a butterfly garden, historic icehouse, and smokehouse.

Tours/Programs: Outstanding programs for all ages include "pet therapy" outreach: visiting hospital pediatric wards, handicap centers, nursing and convalescent homes.

Eating: Picnic tables.

Driving: From Philadelphia, cross Delaware River on Ben Franklin or Walt Whitman Bridge and pick up I-295 North to Mount Holly. Take Route 38 North to first light, go right onto Hartford Road to first stop sign. Left onto Hainesport Road, and go half a mile. Park in lot and walk down dirt drive.

Peace Valley Nature Center

170 Chapman Road, R.D. 1
Doylestown, PA 18901
(215) 345-7860

Hours: Trails open daily, dawn to dusk. Gift shop and solar house open Tuesday-Sunday, 9 AM-5 PM. Closed Mondays and holidays.

Cost: Free.

Description: Beautiful grounds, very good educational programs. Nature Center has a working solar addition and library.

Eating: Snack bar and picnic areas.

Driving: PA Turnpike to exit 27 (Willow Grove). Follow Route 611 North into Doylestown. Turn left onto Route 313 West, go for approximately 2 miles and turn left onto New Galena Road, then left again onto Chapman Road.

Pennypack Environmental Center

8600 Verree Road
Philadelphia, PA 19115
(215) 685-0470

Hours: Trails, dawn to dusk. Indoor exhibit hours vary, call ahead.

Cost: Free. (There is a fee for groups.)

Description: 100-acre nature sanctuary with over 2 miles of trails, located at the western end of 1600-acre Pennypack Park. The small indoor center includes aquariums and displays on local wildlife. Near the building are a bird blind, herb garden, compost and campfire areas.

Tours/Programs: 50 public programs, workshops, campfires, craft sessions, and festivals. Four festivals a year at nearby Fox Chase Farm featuring sheepshearing, Applefest, Family Farm Day, and maple sugaring.

Eating: Picnic tables.

Pool Wildlife Sanctuary

3701 Orchid Place
Emmaus, PA 18049
(610) 965-4397   & ⚓

Hours: Monday-Friday, 9 AM-3 PM; Sunday, 12 noon-4 PM. Closed major holidays. Trails open daily, dawn to dusk.

Cost: Voluntary donations.

Description: Good trail guides lead visitors through shady and sunny habitats in the sanctuary. Environmental Education Center has rocks and minerals, tree and nest exhibit, and more.

Tours/Programs: Family programs.

Eating: Picnic tables.

Driving: PA Turnpike to the Northeast Extension. At exit 33 (Lehigh Valley), go east on Route 22, then south on Route 309, getting off at Cedar Crest Boulevard exit. Go right at the exit onto Cedar Crest Boulevard. Go 2 miles, then take a left on Riverbend Road, right on Orchid Place. Watch for old stone barn with red door and the sanctuary on your right.

Rancocas Nature Center

Rancocas Road, R.D. 1
Mount Holly, NJ 08060
(609) 261-2495   🚐 🔔

Hours: Tuesday-Sunday, 9 AM-5 PM. Closed Mondays and major holidays.

Cost: Free.

Description: Part of New Jersey Audubon Society park system. Small nature center with exhibits and hands-on material. Short, very well-marked outdoor trail with interesting, instructive trail guide.

Tours/Programs: New Jersey Audubon system programs.

Driving: From Philadelphia, cross Delaware River to New Jersey, take Route I-295 North across Rancocas Creek. Take exit 45A (Willingboro/Mount Holly) and follow Rancocas Road for 1 1/2 miles. Nature Center is on your right.

Riverbend Environmental Education Center
Box 2, Springmill Road
Gladwyne, PA 19035
(610) 527-5234

Hours: Monday-Friday, 9 AM-5 PM; Saturday-Sunday, 10 AM-4 PM.

Cost: Free.

Description: 26 acres of land include a stone farm house, working water wheel, springhouse, barn, and bird viewing area. Two miles of trails stimulate curiosity and enthusiasm for the environment. Riverbend also owns two small properties in Rosemont and Merion Station which are open to the public. Call for information.

Tours/Programs: Many programs and special events for children, school groups, and for teachers. Call for newsletter and schedule of events. Fun Saturday and summer programs.

Driving: I-76 (Schuylkill Expressway) West to Conshohocken exit. Go right at the light onto Front Street. Follow signs for Route 23 (Conshohocken State Road). Go left on Spring Mill Road, pass Philadelphia Country Club. Nature Center parking lot is at the end of Spring Mill.

Robbins Park for Environmental Studies
1419 East Butler Pike
Ambler, PA 19002
(215) 641-0921

Hours: Open daily, dawn to dusk.

Cost: Park free. Fee for programs.

Description: Forty-acre park features a variety of well-marked trails, nature talks, crafts, and interpretive programs for all ages and abilities. Enthusiastic staff loves to take visitors around, showing the bird blind, totem pole, log cabin museum, solar greenhouse, small animals, and more. Lots of summer programs for kids; year-round programs for scouts, school groups, etc.

Eating: Picnics allowed. Recycling encouraged.

Driving: PA Turnpike to exit 26 (Fort Washington). Take first right onto 309 North to second exit (Butler Pike/Susquehanna). Down ramp, turn left, go to the first traffic light, then right onto Butler Pike. Go under Route 309 and look for a log cabin and newer pavilion on the left just beyond Temple Ambler Campus sign on the right. Approximately at Butler Pike and Meetinghouse Road.

Schuylkill Center for Environmental Education

Hagy's Mill Road
Philadelphia, PA 19128
(215) 482-7300

Hours: Monday-Saturday, 8:30 AM-5 PM; Sunday, 1 PM-5 PM.

Cost: $3.00 adults, $2.00 children under 12.

Description: Within the city limits, SCEE boasts 500 acres of nature trails, streams, ponds, forests, and wildlife habitats. Large Education Building has spacious young child's Discovery Room with multitude of fun activities, outstanding bookstore/gift shop, and a wide variety of quality programs for all ages. Visit their new seasonal outdoor butterfly house and children's natural history library.

Tours/Programs: Family programs offered every weekend. Special holiday programs blend natural crafts with seasonal themes.

Eating: Picnic area.

Driving: I-76 (Schuylkill Expressway) West to Belmont Avenue exit. Cross bridge into Manayunk and continue straight up the hill on Green Lane. At the top, take a left onto Ridge Avenue. Go 2 miles, turn left onto Port Royal Avenue, then right onto Hagy's Mill Road. Nature center is on the left.

Silver Lake Nature Center

1006 Bath Road
Bristol, PA 19007
(215) 785-1177

Hours: Tuesday-Saturday, 10 AM-5 PM; Sunday, 12 noon-5 PM.

Cost: Free.

Description: Part of the Bucks County park system, Silver Lake has 2 miles of trails. Bird observation in converted garage, "please touch" table, and variety of frogs, turtles, and fish.

Eating: Picnic tables.

Driving: PA Turnpike to exit 27 (Delaware Valley). Take Route 13 South to second light. Turn right on Bath Road. Pass Lower Bucks Hospital. Nature Center is on right.

Welkinweir Preserve

7 Prizer Road
Pottstown, PA 19464
(610) 469-6366

Hours: Dawn to dusk.

Cost: Free.

Description: Plant and animal sanctuary managed by the Natural Lands Trust, Inc. Programs for children available by calling Taylor Arboretum (215-876-2649). Otherwise, this beautiful old estate is great for a casual walk.

Driving: PA Turnpike to exit 23 (Downingtown). Take Route 100 North to Prizer Road, then go west on Prizer Road for about half a mile to second driveway on left.

Planetariums and Observatories

Call ahead for hours and cost. All have instructors to assist, and offer programs for school groups.

Eastern College Planetarium & Observatory

St. Davids, PA 19085
(610) 341-5945

Special holiday show at the Planetarium about Star of David.

Fels Planetarium

Franklin Institute
20th Street and Ben Franklin Parkway
Philadelphia, PA 19103
(215) 448-1200

Haverford College Observatory

Walton Road
Haverford, PA 19041
(610) 896-1333

New Jersey State Museum and Planetarium

See New Jersey State Museum, page 66.

North Museum Planetarium
See North Museum, page 167.

Reading Public Museum Planetarium
See Reading Public Museum, page 70 (school groups only).

Sproul Observatory
Swarthmore College
Swarthmore, PA 19081
(610) 328-8272

Villanova University Observatory
4th Floor, Mendel Hall
Villanova, PA 19085
(610) 519-4820

Zoos

Brandywine Zoo
1001 North Park Drive
Wilmington, DE 19802
(302) 571-7747

Hours: Daily 10 AM-4 PM.

Cost: April-October: $3.00 adults, $1.50 children 3-11 and seniors, under 3 free. November-March: everyone free.

Description: Small, compact, and clean. Good variety of animals in well-planned, naturalistic habitats built on the side of a hill. Otter exhibit is especially fun. Located in Brandywine Park.

Time Needed: 1 hour.

Tours/Programs: Tours available upon request; special programs throughout the year. "Adopt-an-animal" opportunities.

Eating: Snack bar, picnic area.

Driving: I-95 South toward Wilmington. Exit at Concord Pike (Route 202). Follow 202 South to second light, bear right onto Baynard Boulevard. Take Baynard to 18th Street, right onto 18th, right at first stop sign. Left at sign for Zoo. Park on the street.

Cape May County Park and Zoo

707 Route 9, North
Cape May Court House, NJ 08210
(609) 465-5271

Hours: Daily 10 AM-5 PM. Closed Christmas.

Cost: Free (donations welcome).

Description: This wonderful 25-acre zoo features more than 300 animals, a Reptile House, and the new African Savanna project. Nature lovers can explore woodland trails, fish in the pond, or enjoy the bike trails throughout the surrounding 200-acre park. Visit the new "World of Birds" aviary featuring exotic birds.

Time Needed: 1 hour.

Eating: Concession stand open in summer and on weekends in fall and spring. Picnic tables scattered throughout zoo.

Directions: In New Jersey, take the Garden State Parkway south to exit 11. Turn right onto Cresthaven Road and go straight into zoo.

Cohanzick Zoo

See Bridgeton, page 149.

Elmwood Park Zoo

Harding Boulevard
Norristown, PA 19401
(610) 277-DUCK (3825)

Hours: Daily 10 AM-4 PM. Closed Thanksgiving, Christmas, and New Year's Day.

Cost: $3.50 adults, $2.00 seniors and children ages 3-12, under 3 free.

Description: Excellent, small, manageable zoo for young children which provides a close-up look at cougars, bears, birds of prey, and other North American animals including bison and elk. Don't miss the Amish barn with the very friendly, and always hungry, farm animals.

Time Needed: 1 hour.

Tours/Programs: Workshops available for groups and sometimes on summer weekends. Special programs in small amphitheater.

Eating: Snack bar and picnic tables.

(*continued on next page*)

Driving: I-76 (Schuylkill Expressway) West to Route 202 North, past The Court at King of Prussia. Do not take Bridgeport exit off Route 202. Continue straight after the exit to Harding Boulevard. Take left onto Harding and go about half a mile. Zoo is on the left.

Philadelphia Zoo
(The Philadelphia Zoological Garden)

3400 West Girard Avenue
Philadelphia, PA 19104
(215) 243-1100

Hours: Monday-Friday, 9:30 AM-5 PM; Saturday, Sunday and holidays, 9:30 AM-6 PM. Closed Thanksgiving, Christmas Eve, Christmas Day, New Year's Eve, and New Year's Day.

Cost: $10.50 ages 12 and up, $8.00 seniors and children 5-11, $5.00 children 2-4, under 2 free.

Description: With over 2,000 animals, America's First Zoo always has something going on. The Reptile House features King Cobra's Temple and the primate reserve is home to over 40 animals ranging from the 400-pound gorilla to the 1/4-pound pygmy marmoset. Don't miss the underwater polar bear exhibit, the African Plains, and the Children's Zoo with many animal shows.

Time Needed: 3 hours up to a full, fun day.

Tours/Programs: Group tours available through Docent Office. Highly recommended workshops and special events throughout the year. Night Flight Programs invite you to spend the night at the Zoo and explore it when the animals love it best.

Eating: McDonald's with indoor and outdoor tables. Snack bars and picnic areas throughout the zoo.

Driving: I-76 (Schuylkill Expressway) West to Girard Avenue exit and follow signs to the Zoo. Parking available on 34th Street or Girard Avenue. Public transportation available.

The largest mammal native to Pennsylvania is the elk which can weigh up to 800 lbs. The smallest is the pygmy shrew which weighs as much as a dime.

Trexler Lehigh Game Preserve

5150 Game Preserve Road
Schnecksville, PA 18078
(610) 799-4171
www.lehighvalleyzoo.org

Hours: May-October: daily 10 AM-5 PM (gate closes at 4 PM).

Cost: $5.00 adults, $3.00 seniors, $3.00 children under 13.

Description: Nestled in a 1400-acre game preserve, this 28-acre zoo is a great adventure. Pick up a packet at the education center and set off as Carmen Sandiego to find clues to solve the zoo's various mysteries. Be sure to watch for elk and bison on your way out.

Time Needed: 1 hour.

Tours/Programs: Special programs throughout the year include a Butterfly Festival and Zoo Olympics.

Eating: Concession stand.

Directions: Route 476 North (Blue Route) to Route 22 East to Route 309 North. Stay on Route 309 North for 5.6 miles. Turn left at Game Preserve sign onto Game Preserve Road. Entrance is 2 miles on left.

Zoo America

See Hershey, page 159.

Performing Arts

Every child loves the magic of a stage performance, no matter which side of the lights he or she is on. The performing groups listed here put on programs specifically for children. Most groups have matinee performances, and with the exception of the glorious *Nutcracker*, most tickets are inexpensive.

The Annenberg Center's giant annual children's festival in late May offers a mind-boggling array of international talent—singing, dancing, miming, and performing magnificently just for children. The Annenberg Center is at 3680 Walnut Street, Philadelphia, PA 19104; call (215) 898-6791 for information and reservations.

Don't forget to check out the local radio and TV, particularly "Kid's Corner" with Kathy O'Connell on WXPN.

Dance

National Ballet Company of New Jersey

5113 Church Road
Mount Laurel, NJ 08054
(609) 235-5342

A variety of dance performances for children through the year.

Pennsylvania Ballet Company

1101 South Broad Street
Philadelphia, PA 19147
(215) 551-7014

Children are entranced by the classic *Nutcracker* at the Academy of Music during the holiday season.

Philadelphia Civic Ballet Company

1615 Sansom Street
Philadelphia, PA 19103
(215) 564-1505
(610) 544-3709 (suburban performances)

One performance just for children each season at varying locations. Special children's holiday performance at the Free Library.

Temple University's Conwell Dance Theater

Dance Department, Seltzer Hall, 3rd Floor
Temple University
Philadelphia, PA 19122
(215) 204-8414

Young People's Performance Series of approximately five matinees places emphasis on audience participation.

Music

Haddonfield Symphony

P.O. Box 212
30 Washington Street
Haddonfield, NJ 08033
(609) 429-1880

Two children's concerts, one in the fall and one in the spring.

Philadelphia Boys Choir and Chorale

225 North 32nd Street
Philadelphia, PA 19104
(215) 222-3500

About 80 boys, ages 8-13, sing with extraordinary beauty at more than 40 performances each year.

Philadelphia Orchestra's Family Concerts

Academy of Music
Broad and Locust Streets
Philadelphia, PA 19103
(215) 893-1955

Short, lively performances with quick lessons well-camouflaged and easy to digest.

Settlement Music School Recitals

416 Queen Street
Philadelphia, PA 19147
(215) 336-0400

Student or teacher recitals each month, in each of five branches throughout the city. Watch for special performances during the year on a single subject, such as jazz.

Local Radio and TV

RADIO

"Kid's Corner" on WXPN (88.5 FM)

University of Pennsylvania
3905 Spruce Street
Philadelphia, PA 19104
(215) 898-6677

Monday-Friday, 7 PM-8 PM. Exciting live call-in show for 6 to 12 year olds dealing with many issues ranging from questions about your computer to how to deal with your parents getting divorced. Call line: 1-800-KIDS-XPN.

TELEVISION

"Al Albert's Showcase" on WPVI-TV 6

4100 City Line Avenue
Philadelphia, PA 19131
(609) 889-2232

Children's talent show, Saturday, 12 noon.

"Kidtime News" on WPHL-TV 17

5001 Wynnefield Avenue
Philadelphia, PA 19131
(215) 878-1700

Sixty-second vignette series airs twice a day. Middle school and high school students participate through the Philadelphia school system.

The state dog of Pennsylvania is the great dane, one of William Penn's favorite pets and a popular hunting and working breed during the frontier times.

Theater and Theatrical Fun

Plays, puppets, clowns, and films for children.

American Family Theater
Penn's Landing
Philadelphia, PA
(215) 629-6501

American Theater Arts for Youth
1429 Walnut Street
Philadelphia, PA 19102
(215) 563-3501, or 1-800-523-4540

Annenberg Center Theatre for Children
3680 Walnut Street
Philadelphia, PA 19102
(215) 898-3900

Annual children's festival in late May is fantastic!

Appel Farm Arts
P.O. Box 770
Elmer, NJ 08318
(609) 358-2472 or (800) 394-1211 (ticket line)
(Saturday afternoons, fall and spring)

Bridgeton Theatre in the Park
Amphitheater at Sunset Lake Beach
Bridgeton, NJ 08302
(609) 451-9208
(Wednesday nights in July)

Bristol Riverside Theater
120 Radcliffe Street
Bristol, PA 19007
(215) 788-7827

Bucks County Community College Theater

Cultural Programs Office
Cottage 3
Newtown, PA 18940
(215) 968-8186

Bucks County Playhouse

70 South Main Street
P.O. Box 313
New Hope, PA 18938
(215) 862-2041

Cabrini College Theater for Young People

Upper Gulph Road
Radnor, PA 19087
(610) 902-8510

Camarata Opera Theater

1006 Kingston Drive
Cherry Hill, NJ 08034
(609) 428-7999

Cheltenham Playhouse Children's Theatre

439 Ashbourne Road
Cheltenham, PA 19012
(215) 379-4027

Delaware Children's Theater

1014 Delaware Avenue
Wilmington, DE 19806
(302) 655-1014

350-seat theater with frequent performances. Call for reservations—they sell out quickly.

Footlighters Theater

Berwyn, PA 19312
(610) 296-9245

Forge Theater

342 First Avenue
Phoenixville, PA 19460
(610) 935-1920

Free Library of Philadelphia

1901 Vine Street
Philadelphia, PA 19103-1189
(215) 686-5372

Book concerts, magicians, music, ballet, and other dance groups, films, and plays. Many interpreted in sign language.

Fulton Opera House

12 North Prince Street
P.O. Box 1865
Lancaster, PA 17603
(717) 397-7425

Family holiday performance in December. Touring group for schools, February-May.

Grand Opera House

818 North Market Street Mall
Wilmington, DE 19801
(302) 658-7897

Haddonfield Plays & Players

P.O. Box 145
Haddonfield, NJ 08033
(609) 429-8139

Hedgerow Theater

64 Rose Valley Road
Rose Valley, PA 19080
(610) 565-4211

Immaculata College Theater

Alumni Hall
Immaculata, PA 19345
(610) 647-4400

Keswick Theater

291 Keswick Avenue
Glenside, PA 19038
(215) 572-7650

Marple Newtown Players

20 Media Line Road
Newtown Square, PA 19073
(610) 353-9181

Meagher Theater at Newman College

Utz Center
Concord Road
Aston, PA 19014
(610) 558-5626

Media Theatre for the Performing Arts

104 East State Street
Media, PA 19063
(610) 566-4020 or (800) 568-7771

Montgomery County Community College Theater

340 DeKalb Pike
Blue Bell, PA 19422
(215) 641-6505

New Freedom Theater

1346 North Broad Street
Philadelphia, PA 19121
(215) 765-2793

People's Light & Theater Company

39 Conestoga Road
Malvern, PA 19355
(610) 644-3500

Performing Arts Center

Jim Leeds Road
Pomona, NJ 08240
(609) 652-9000

Playhouse Theater

DuPont Building
Wilmington, DE 19801
(302) 656-4401

Plays and Players Children's Theatre

1714 Delancey Place
Philadelphia, PA 19103
(215) 735-0630

Please Touch Museum

Virginia Evans Theater
210 North 21st Street
Philadelphia, PA 19103
(215) 963-0666

Puttin' on the Ritz Children's Theatre

915 White Horse Pike
Oaklyn, NJ 08107
(609) 858-5230

Ronald McDonald Children's Theater

3925 Chestnut Street
Philadelphia, PA 19104
(215) 387-8406

Storybook Musical Theatre
Box 473
Abington, PA 19001
(215) 659-8550

Upper Darby Performing Arts Center
Lansdowne Avenue and School Lane
Drexel Hill, PA 19026
(610) 622-1189

Village Players of Hatboro
P.O. Box 444
Hatboro, PA 19040
(215) 675-6774

Walt Whitman Cultural Arts Center
2nd and Cooper Streets
Camden, NJ 08102
(609) 757-7276

War Memorial Theater
West Lafayette Street
Trenton, NJ 08608
(609) 984-8484

West Chester and Barleysheaf Players
29 Whitford Road
Lionville, PA 19353
(610) 363-7075

Young People's Theatre Workshop
Players Club of Swarthmore
Fairview Road
Swarthmore, PA 19081
(610) 328-4271

Recreation

Active togetherness, whether you're picking apples or tubing down a river, makes happy memories.

The recreational activities listed here are those I find appeal most to children. If I've missed your child's favorite, please send me information so I can include it in the next edition.

Amusement Parks

Hours and costs change frequently, so it's best to call ahead. If you are an AAA member, some places will give you a discount.

Clementon Amusement Park & Splashworld Water Park

144 Berlin Road
Clementon, NJ 08021
(609) 783-0263   ♿

Hours: July-August: Wednesday-Sunday, 12 noon-8 PM (WaterPark), 12 noon-10 PM (Amusement Park).

Cost: $20.95 for all ages, both parks ($16.95 if after 4 PM). Under 36 inches free.

Description: Lots of rides for all ages; nothing scary for even the youngest visitor. Magicians and clowns throughout the park.

Eating: Covered pavilions for picnics; many concession stands.

Driving: Walt Whitman Bridge to New Jersey, then go south on Route 42. Get off at Blackwood/Clementon exit, then follow Route 534 East. Entrance to park is 4 miles ahead on the right.

Dorney Park and Wildwater Kingdom

3830 Dorney Park Road
Allentown, PA 18104
(610) 395-2000   ♿
www.dorneypark.com

Hours: Park: May-August and weekends Labor Day-October: Monday-Friday, 10 AM-10 PM; Saturday-Sunday, 10 AM-10 PM. Wildwater Kingdom: Memorial Day-June, 10 AM-6 PM; July-August: 10 AM-8 PM. (Evening hours are subject to change. I recommend calling ahead.)

Cost: $31.00 adults (over 4 feet tall) for both parks; $7.00 under 4 feet tall and seniors; under 4 free. (Reduced adult rates on special weekends; call for schedule.)

Description: Dorney Park is the dry side, Wildwater Kingdom is not. Dorney is for all ages, with easy rides for young ones up to gravity-defying roller coasters like the Steel Force and the Dominator Tower for fearless teens. Berenstain Bear Country

(*continued on next page*)

appeals to the very youngest who love to meet the bear characters and frolic through interactive games, both indoors and out.

Eating: Plenty of food available everywhere. Picnic pavilions for groups can be reserved ahead of time.

Driving: PA Turnpike to the Northeast Extension to exit 33 (Lehigh Valley). Follow Route 22 East to Route 309 South to Hamilton Boulevard (Route 222). Go left off the exit ramp and follow signs for the parks.

Dutch Wonderland

2249 Lincoln Highway East
Lancaster, PA 17602
(717) 291-1888

Hours: Mid-April-Memorial Day: Saturday, 10 AM-6 PM; Sunday, 11 AM-6 PM. June: daily 10 AM-6 PM. July-August: daily 10 AM-8 PM. September-mid-October: Saturday, 10 AM-6 PM; Sunday, 11 AM-6 PM.

Cost: $22.50 ages 7-59, $17.50 children 3-6, $16.00 seniors, under 3 free.

Description: Perfect amusement park for younger children. Over 25 rides including a watercoaster, boats, trains, a double-splash floam ride, two roller coasters, and a family parachute ride. Monorail around the park (additional charge). The high dive demonstration, botanical garden, and animated show catch the attention of all ages.

Eating: Food stands and picnic tables.

Driving: PA Turnpike West to exit 21 (Reading), then 222 South to Route 30 East. Stay on Route 30 for 5 miles, big castle-like structure on left.

Eagle Falls

2343 Lincoln Highway East (Route 30)
Lancaster, PA 17602
(717) 397-4674

Hours: Adventure Golf: weekends in May, September, and October, 10 AM-10 PM. Memorial Day weekend-Labor Day (weather permitting): water activities, 12 noon-7 PM; Adventure Golf, 12 noon-10 PM.

(*continued on next page*)

Cost: $13.50 unlimited rides and golf, $12.00 unlimited rides, $9.00 for 12 rides. Go-carts: $4.00 for four minutes for the junior carts; $5.00 for five minutes for the Grand Prix (or $1.00 as a passenger).

Description: Two water slides for adults and one for children. Everyone must go down slides alone. Championship miniature adventure golf covers 1 1/2 acres, 18-hole course complete with caves, waterfalls, and lots of fun. Two go-cart tracks, one for ages 5-9 and the Grand Prix for those 52 inches or taller.

Eating: Snack bar, ice cream parlor, picnic area.

Driving: PA Turnpike West to exit 23 (Downington). Go south on Route 100, then west on Route 30 to just past Route 896. Eagle Falls is on the right.

HersheyPark

See Hershey, page 158.

Sesame Place

Oxford Valley Road
Langhorne, PA 19407
(215) 757-1100 recorded, or 752-7070

Hours: April-May: Saturday-Sunday, 10 AM-5 PM; May-June: 10 AM-5 PM; July-August: 9 AM-8 PM; early September: 10 AM-5 PM; September-October: Saturday-Sunday, 10 AM-5 PM.

Cost: $29.95 per person, $26.95 seniors, $19.95 after 5 PM, under 2 free. Parking charge: $6.00.

Description: Rides and attractions feature Bert, Ernie, and the gang, but activities also abound for children up to age 13 including the Vapor Trail roller coaster. Outdoor climbing and jumping, indoor see-yourself-on-television broadcasts, computer games, and more. There are some exciting water games, so visitors should have bathing suits on under their clothes and wear shoes that are easy to take off and put on several times.

Eating: Picnic tables and cafeteria with healthy kid food.

Driving: I-95 North to exit 29A. Take Route 1 North to Oxford Valley exit, right on Oxford Valley Road, right at second light to park.

Six Flags Great Adventure

Route 537
P.O. Box 120
Jackson, NJ 08527
(732) 928-1821   &

Hours: 10 AM-10 PM daily in summer. Hours vary in May, June and after Labor Day.

Cost: Theme park and Safari: $45.75 adults, $22.90 children, $26.50 seniors. Theme park only: $44.70 adults, $22.35 children, $25.45 seniors. Safari only: $15.90 all ages. Under 3 free.

Description: Everyone enjoys the wild rides in the big theme park, but don't forget to visit the Wild Safari Animal Park too. 1200 animals roam through 350 acres. Bugs Bunny Land has 25 rides for the youngest visitors.

Eating: Food available everywhere. Picnic areas near Safari entrance and bus parking lot outside main entrance.

Driving: NJ Turnpike to exit 7A, east on I-95 for 12 miles to exit 16 (Mount Holly-Freehold). Watch for signs.

Storybook Land

Black Horse Pike
Cardiff, NJ 08232
(609) 641-7847   &

Hours: Summer, daily 10 AM-5:30 PM. Call for hours in late spring and October-December.

Cost: $11.50 per person, under 1 free.

Description: Rides for even the youngest of Mother Goose's friends—merry-go-rounds, small cars, Flying Jumbo, and a small train to ride. Fun to feed the live animals which include sheep and goats. This park, with its many shade trees, is unexpectedly pleasant on hot days. More than 90,000 lights brighten the area at Christmas time.

Eating: Plenty available.

Driving: From Philadelphia, cross to New Jersey and follow I-676 South to Route 422 South to Route 322 South (Black Horse Pike) to Cardiff. Watch for white castle-like structure.

Harvesting

One of the outings children are eager to repeat year after year is harvesting, whether it's picking apples from dwarf trees or cutting their own evergreen tree for the holiday season. Prices fluctuate, as do hours of operation and crops available for harvesting. I recommend you call before going.

Christmas Tree Cutting

DELAWARE
New Castle County
Coleman's Tree Farm, Odessa (302) 378-8949

NEW JERSEY
Burlington County
Axten's Tree Farm, Marlton (609) 985-1835
Beaver's Farm, Wrightstown (609) 298-2516
Charles D. Wesner, Medford Lakes (609) 654-8847
Chesterfield Tree Farm, Chesterfield (609) 298-3234
DeCou's Christmas Trees, Moorestown (609) 234-6113
Emmons Tree Farm, Pemberton (609) 894-8142
Fernbrook Nursery, Bordentown (609) 298-8282
Gravely Pond, Medford (609) 953-0511
Haines Tree Farm, Juliustown (609) 894-2967
Haines Tree Farm, Burlington (609) 877-0695
Indian Acres Tree Farm, Medford (609) 953-0087

Kemlin Tree Farm, Edgewater Park (609) 829-6549
Riley's Tree Farm, Medford (609) 654-4434
Train Tree Plantation, Lumberton (609) 261-4444
Wading River Christmas Tree Farm, Wading River (609) 965-0194
Worth & Sharp Christmas Tree Farm, Tabernacle (609) 268-8455

Camden County
Brown Tree Farm, Sicklerville (609) 561-0913
Peter P. Lucca, Berlin (609) 767-0189

Cumberland County
McDermott's Christmas Trees, Bridgeton (609) 451-0747

Gloucester County
Belly Acres Christmas Tree Farm, Franklinville (609) 694-0350
Exley's Country Lane Nursery, Sewell (609) 468-5949
Grace Tree Farm Inc., Vineland (609) 692-3432
Gypsy Run Tree Farm, Glassboro (609) 881-5450
Hanks' Christmas Tree Ranch, Mullica Hill (609) 478-4243
LB's Trees, Mullica Hill (609) 694-2875, (800) 858-2366
Pek's Trees, Elk Township (609) 881-0198
Robert's Nursery, Turnersville (609) 582-1989
Stecher's Country Store, Swedesboro (609) 467-2208
Triple Oaks Nursery, Franklinville (609) 694-4272

Mercer County
Bear Swamp Christmas Tree Farm, Trenton (609) 587-1411

Salem County
Ralph Battle, Monroeville (609) 358-2820
Stimpson's Tree Farm, Monroeville (609) 358-2384

PENNSYLVANIA
Bucks County
Bryan's Farm, Richboro (215) 598-3206
Evergreen Christmas Tree Farm, Silverdale (215) 257-1700
Evergreenery, Doylestown (215) 345-9188
Fisher's Christmas Tree Farm, Yardley (215) 493-3563
Gold Mine Christmas Tree Farm, Sellersville (215) 257-5105
Holiday Christmas Tree Farm, (Mechanicsville) Buckingham
    Township (215) 794-7655
Indian Walk Tree Farm, Wrightstown (215) 598-3518
McArdle Tree Farm, Mechanicsville (215) 794-7655
None Such Farm, Buckingham Township (215) 794-5200/5201
Pine Tree Farm, Doylestown (215) 348-0632
Rushton Tree Farm, Pipersville (610) 294-9144
Snipes Farm and Nursery, Morrisville (215) 295-3092
Tinicum Village Tree Farm, Pipersville (215) 297-0445
Top of the Hill Farm, Plumstead Township (215) 345-7949

Tryon Farm, Sellersville (215) 257-6595
Tuckamony Farm, New Hope (215) 297-5054/8447
Watson Tree Farm, Warrington (215) 343-6561
Winterberry Christmas Tree Farm, Pipersville
 (215) 297-8330, (800) 336-8330 - evening

Chester County
Bernard's Tree Farm, Honeybrook (610) 942-4454
Brandywine Valley Association, West Chester (610) 793-1090
Chester Springs Tree Farm, Chester Springs (610) 827-7003
The Farmer in Lyndell, Lyndell (610) 942-9622, or (610) 384-2088
Grigson Farm, Downingtown/West Chester (610) 269-5413
High's Nursery, Pottstown (610) 323-0293
Irish Green Nursery, Avondale (610) 436-8989
Pine Hill Farm, Pottstown (610) 323-8045
Pond View Tree Farm, Kennett Square (610) 444-6046
Shamrock Tree Farm, Pomeroy (610) 857-1048
Stubles' Christmas Trees, Kennett Square (610) 347-2133
Windridge Farm, Chester Springs (610) 469-9299
Windswept Farm, Honeybrook (610) 273-3032
Yeager's Farm, Phoenixville (610) 933-7379

Delaware County
Indian Orchards, Media (610) 565-8387
Smallbrook Farm, Evergreen Nursery, Glen Mills (610) 459-3631

Lehigh County
Kohler's Tree Farm, East Greenville (215) 679-6588

Montgomery County
Boswell's Tree Farm, Skippack Township (610) 584-4739
Buck Nursery, Pennsburg (215) 679-6603
F & H Tree Farm, Collegeville/Trappe (610) 667-0483/664-0426
Hague's Christmas Trees, Hatfield (215) 368-4542
Tom's Trees, Royersford (610) 948-8111
Varner's Tree Farm, Collegeville (610) 489-8878

Pick Your Own
(*Hayrides offered at some farms*)

DELAWARE
New Castle County
Gerald Zeh, Middletown (302) 378-2840
 Strawberries: end May-June
Lovett Farms, Middletown (302) 378-2120/9393
 Strawberries: end May-June
Powell Farms, Townsend (302) 378-8058
 Strawberries: end May-June

Pulaski's Produce, Middletown (302) 378-2754
Tomatoes: mid-July through September; pumpkins: end
September-October; peas: June

Valley Brook Farm, Townsend (302) 378-2409
Strawberries: end May-June

Warner Enterprises, Milford (302) 422-9506
Strawberries: end May-June; peas: June

NEW JERSEY
Burlington County

Bud Wells Blueberries, Vincentown (609) 726-1116
Blueberries: July

Conte Farms, Tabernacle (609) 268-1010
Strawberries: June; string beans: mid-June through August; peaches:
August; blueberries: July; red raspberries: July-August; tomatoes, peppers:
July-September; apples: September; pumpkins: October

Edward Wells blueberries, Vincentown (609) 859-2662
Blueberries: July

Four Winds Farm, Tabernacle (609) 268-9113
Strawberries: June; blueberries: end June; blackberries: mid-July through
mid-August; red raspberries: mid-August through first frost; pumpkins:
October; mums: July-August; apples: end August

Fred and III, Pemberton (609) 894-2198
Blueberries: July through mid-August

Giberson's Blueberries, Vincentown (609) 859-3634
Blueberries: July through mid-August

Griffin Farm, Pemberton (609) 894-2915
Blueberries: July through mid-August

Johnson's Corner Farm, Medford (609) 654-8643
Asparagus: late April-May; strawberries: end May-June; corn, flowers:
July-August; peaches: August; pumpkins, Indian corn and gourds:
September-Halloween; popcorn, peanuts: November

Katona Farms Inc., Crosswicks (609) 298-3342
Tomatoes: Mid-July through Mid-September; sweet corn: end June

North Branch Blueberries, Brown Mills (609) 893-5693
Blueberries: July

Orchard Lane Farm, Chesterfield (609) 259-3684
   Strawberries, peas: May-June; raspberries, string beans: July; peaches,
   bush limas: July through August; apples: September-October

Piper Blueberry Farm, Pemberton (609) 894-9227
   Blueberries: July

Reeves Blueberry Farm, New Lisbon (609) 894-2171/8168
   Blueberries: July

River Side Homestead Farm, Cinnaminson (609) 829-4992
   (All organically grown)
   Peas: June; snap beans: mid-June through mid-July; tomatoes, eggplant:
   mid-July through September; peaches: mid-July through August; peppers:
   mid-July through October; pears: August; apples: September-October;
   pumpkins: October

Robson Farm, Wrightstown (609) 758-2068/2566/2577
   Strawberries: June

Russell Grover's Farm, Pemberton (609) 894-8171
   Blueberries: July

Sharp Farm, Pemberton (609) 894-8152
   Blueberries: end June-July

Springville Orchard, Mount Laurel (609) 235-5488
   Apples: end August-October

Strawberry Hill Farm, Chesterfield (609) 298-0823
   Apples: September-October; peaches: mid-August; pumpkins:
   September-October

Tom Haines Blueberries, Pemberton (609) 894-8630
   Blueberries: July

Warren Ash, Pemberton (609) 894-2428
   Blueberries: July

Worrell Blueberries, Chatsworth (609)726-9236
   Blueberries:July

Camden County
Springdale Farms, Cherry Hill (609) 424-8674
   Strawberries: June; string beans: July; pole lima beans: mid-July
   through August; flowers: mid-July to mid-September

Cumberland County
Nate Bisconte Farm, Rosenhayn (609) 455-3405
   Strawberries: June

Sidney Rassas, Millville (609) 451-3920
   Blueberries: July

Gloucester County
Cedarvale Farms, Repaupo (609) 467-2832/3550
   Strawberries: end of May through early June

Duffield's Farm Market, Sewell (609) 589-7090
Peas, strawberries: June

Fruitwood Orchards, Hardingville (609) 881-7748
Raspberries: mid-June through mid-July, September; peaches: mid-July through August; sour cherries: mid-June through mid-July; apples: mid-August through October

Mood's Farm Market, Mullica Hill (609) 478-2500
Sweet and pie cherries: June; blueberries, string beans, plums, peaches, nectarines: July; raspberries: July-September; blackberries, blue plums, pears: August; grapes: August-September; apples: September

Patane's Farm, Gibbstown (609) 423-2726
Squash: mid-June through August; string beans: June-July; tomatoes: mid-July through mid-September; peppers: mid-July through October; eggplants: mid-July through September; cucumbers: July through mid-August; cantaloupes: July-August; watermelons: August; turnip greens: September-October

Tuck-A-Lou Orchards, Hardingville (609) 881-0582/0393
Strawberries, peas: June; blueberries, thornless blackberries, raspberries: July; peaches: mid-July through August; apples: September-October; mums, pumpkins: October

U-Pick, Mullica Hill (609) 478-2864
Peaches: mid-July through August; eggplant: mid-July through September; okra: mid-August through mid-September; apples: September-October

Mercer County
Grover Farm, Princeton Junction (609) 799-1195
Strawberries, peas: June; green beans, lima beans: July; potatoes, sweet corn: July-August; pumpkins, gourds: October

Lee Turkey Farm, Hightstown (609) 448-0629
Peas, strawberries, lettuce: mid-May through June; cherries: June; spinach, rhubarb, tomatoes, beans: July; apples: July-October; peaches: mid-July through August; eggplant, peppers, green beans: mid-July through October; zucchini, flowers, cucumbers: mid-July to frost; broccoli, cabbage, cauliflower, okra, collards, raspberries, pumpkins: September-October

Terhune Orchards, Princeton (609) 924-2310
Sour cherries: June; peaches: mid-July through August; blueberries, raspberries: July; apples: September-October

Tindall Farm, Trenton (609) 426-1123
Strawberries: June

Salem County
Daniel L. Sauder Farm, Norma (609) 692-9424
Strawberries, peas: June; string beans: July

Larchmont Farms, Elmer (609) 358-0700/3454
Cherries: June; apples: September-October

Nichols Orchards, Norma (609) 694-0986
Summer apples, peaches, nectarines: mid-July through August

William Jenkins, Pedricktown (609) 299-4346
Strawberries: end May-June

PENNSYLVANIA
Bucks County
Fairview Farms, Pineville (215) 598-3257
Strawberries, peas: June; string beans: June-August; lima beans: August

Jacob & Jayne Wildemore, Chalfont (215) 249-3683
Strawberries: June; blueberries: July; raspberries: end August; peaches: July-August

None Such Farm, Buckingham (215) 794-5200/5201
Strawberries, peas: June; string beans: end June-September; blackberries: July; raspberries: July, September to frost; tomatoes: mid-July to frost; lima beans: end July to frost; pumpkins: October

Penn Vermont Fruit Farms, Bedminster (215) 795-2475
Strawberries: June; red and black raspberries: July; blackberries: end July-August

Shady Brook Farm, Yardley (215) 968-1670
Strawberries, peas: June; pumpkins: October

Shelly and Hellerick Farm, Curley Hill (215) 766-8388
Strawberries: June; pumpkins: October

Snipes Farm, Morrisville (215) 295-3092
Raspberries: July, September to frost; apples: September to mid-October; strawberries: June

Solly Brothers Market, Ivyland (215) 357-2850
Strawberries, peas: June; green beans: June-August; tomatoes: July; pumpkins: weekends in October; raspberries: August

Trauger's Farm Market, Kintnersville (610) 847-5702
Strawberries: June; string beans: June; peas: June

Weber Farm, Chalfont (215) 343-0169
Strawberries: June; pumpkins: weekends in October; sugar snap peas, shell peas: June

Chester County
Barnard's Orchards, Kennett Square (610) 347-2151
Peaches: August-early September; apples: September-October; pumpkins: October

Highland Orchards, Thorndale (610) 269-3494
Rhubarb: May to mid-June; strawberries, peas: June; cherries: mid-June through early July; blueberries: July to mid-August; red raspberries: July-September; blackberries: July; peaches: mid-July through August; plums: mid-July to mid-September; sweet corn: mid-July through

August; peppers: August; tomatoes: end of July to mid-September; apples: July-October; pears, grapes: mid-August to mid-September; nectarines: August; pumpkins: September-October

Milky Way Farm, Chester Springs (610) 363-2390
Pumpkins: weekends in October

Northbrook Orchards, West Chester (610) 793-1210
Strawberries: June; peaches: late July-early September; apples, pumpkins: September-October

Nussex Farms, West Chester (610) 696-1133
Apples: September; pie cherries: end June-early July

Sugartown Strawberries, Malvern (610) 647-0711
Strawberries: June; pumpkins: October

Delaware County
Indian Orchards, Media (610) 565-8387
Raspberries: June; blueberries: June-August; blackberries: July; apples: August-October; grapes, tomatoes, pears: September; Christmas trees: December

Linvilla Orchards, Media (610) 876-7116
Strawberries: June; red raspberries: end June-July; blackberries: mid-July; peaches: July-September; pears, Concord grapes: August-early September; blueberries: end June-early August; apples: July-August; pumpkins: mid-September through October; fall apples: August-October

Lehigh County
Strawberry Acres, Overlook Orchards, Inc., Copley (610) 262-3674
Cherries, strawberries: June; peaches, pears: August; apples: September through mid-October; pumpkins: October

Montgomery County
Freddy Hill Farms, Lansdale (215) 855-1205
Pumpkins: weekends mid-September through October

S-Berry Farm, Frederick (610) 754-7772
Strawberries: June; blackberries: end July; red raspberries: end August-September; peas: June; raspberries: end June

Rides and Tours

NOTE: These lists are for your convenience. We claim no responsibility, nor do we endorse any company.

Hot Air Balloon Rides

Air Ventures
Brandywine Airport
West Chester, PA 19380
(610) 889-9386

Balloonair
Brandywine Airport
West Chester, PA 19380
(610) 527-1190

Lollipop Balloon
Exton Square Mall
Routes 30 and 100
Exton, PA 19341
(610) 827-1610

Magical Mystery Flights
West Chester, PA
(610) 892-0860

Boat, Barge, and Ferry Rides

Canal Boat Rides
P.O. Box 877
Easton, PA 18044
(610) 250-6700

Holiday Boat Tours
401 North Columbus Boulevard
Philadelphia, PA 19123
(215) 629-8687

Liberty Belle Cruises
Penn's Landing
Delaware River at Spruce Street
Philadelphia, PA 19106
(215) 629-1131

New Hope Mule Barge
P.O. Box 164 (Route 232)
New Hope, PA 18938
(215) 862-2842

RiverLink Ferry
Penn's Landing
Delaware River at Spruce Street
Philadelphia, PA 19106
(215) 925-5465

Spirit of Philadelphia
Penn's Landing
Delaware River at Spruce Street
Philadelphia, PA 19106
(215) 923-4962/4993

Bus Tours

These tours run approximately 1-2 hours. See also Trolley Tours, page 139.

**American Heritage
Landmark Tours**
139 Grubb Road
Malvern, PA 19355
(610) 647-4030

Amish Experience
Box N
Bird-in-Hand, PA 17505
(717) 768-8400

**Atwater Kent Museum
Neighborhood Tours**
15 South 7th Street
Philadelphia, PA 19106
(215) 922-3031

Centipede Tours
1315 Walnut Street
Philadelphia, PA 19107
(215) 735-3123

**Foundation for
Architecture**
*1 Penn Center at Suburban
    Station, Suite 1165*
Philadelphia, PA 19103
(215) 569-3187

Philadelphia Tours
719 Dickinson Street
Philadelphia, PA 19147
(215) 636-1666

Horse-Drawn Carriage Tours

Youngsters enjoy the horse as much as the history spiel. With young ones, request a shorter tour—it costs less.

Bucks County
(pick up near cannon in center of town)
Bucks County Carriages, New Hope, PA (215) 862-3582

Lancaster County
Abe's Buggy Rides, Bird-in-Hand, PA (no telephone)
Ed's Buggy Rides, Strasburg, PA (717) 687-0360

Philadelphia
(pick up across the street from Independence Hall)
Philadelphia Carriage Company (215) 922-6840
'76 Carriage Company (215) 923-8516
Society Hill Carriage Company (215) 627-6128

Scenic Train Rides

These are special rides behind steam engines, but even a local train ride is an adventure for a young child.

Blue Mountain and Reading Railroad
Box 425, Hamburg, PA 19526
(610) 562-2102

Middletown and Hummelstown Railroad
136 Brown Street, Middletown, PA 17057
(717) 944-4435

Pioneer Tunnel Coal Mine and Steam Locomotive
See page 179.

Strasburg Railroad
P.O. Box 96, Route 741, Strasburg, PA 17579
(717) 687-7522

Wilmington and Western Railroad
Greenbank Station, Routes 2 and 41, Wilmington, DE 19801
(302) 998-1930

W. K. & S. Railroad
Box 24, Kempton, PA 19529
(610) 756-6469

Trolley Tours

Choo Choo Trolley and American Trolley Tours (215) 333-2119
Hawk Mountain Line (610) 756-6469
Penn's Landing Trolley (215) 757-7444
Philadelphia Trolley Works (215) 925-8687

The following tours are part of the Fairmount Park system; schedules vary. For information about any of these tours, call (215) 763-8100.

Art Museum Shuttle
Christmas Trolley Tour
Germantown Express

Schuylkill Discovery
Town and Country Tours

Walking Tours

Not all walking tours are included because some last too long for most children.

Black History Strolls
Philadelphia, PA
(215) 242-1214

Centipede Tours
1315 Walnut Street
Philadelphia, PA 19107
(215) 735-3123

Ghost Tours of Philadelphia
5th and Chestnut Streets
Philadelphia, PA 19106
(215) 413-1997

Historic Bridgeton
Walking Tour
Routes 49 and 77
Bridgeton, NJ 08302
(609) 451-4802

Lights of Liberty
(see INHP, page 17)

Park House Guide Tours
Philadelphia Museum of Art
26th Street and Ben Franklin Pkwy
Philadelphia, PA 19101
(215) 763-8100

Whenever Tours

Go at your leisure in your own car. Call for maps.

Bucks County Covered Bridges
Bucks County Tourist Commission
152 Swamp Road
Doylestown, PA 18901
(215) 345-4552

Burlington County Historical Loop Tours
Burlington County Cultural and Heritage Commission
49 Rancocas Road
Mount Holly, NJ 08060
(609) 265-5068

Active Sports

NOTE: These lists are for your convenience only. I claim no responsibility, nor do I endorse any company.

Local YMCAs, YWCAs, and related organizations offer many parent-tot classes. Consult your phone directory.

Only sports where adults can participate with children are listed here. "Drop-off" programs are not included.

In Philadelphia, the Department of Recreation, (215) 686-8490, has information about teams, tournaments, outings, and special events in the following sports: baseball, basketball, bicycling, boating, checkers and chess, fishing, golf, hiking, ice skating, jogging, roller skating, sledding, soccer, softball, swimming, tennis, track and field, volleyball.

Baseball

Almost every township has organized baseball for all ages and stages of development. The Challenger Softball Program for mentally and physically handicapped children operates under official Little League auspices. Call your local Little League or headquarters at (717) 326-1921. For extra practice in batting cages, visit:

Burholme Golf
401 W. Cottman Avenue
Philadelphia, PA 19111
(215) 742-2380

Grand Slam USA
23A Roland Avenue
Mount Laurel, NJ 08054
(609) 866-2077

Grand Slam USA
Airport Industries
Reading, PA 19606
(610) 375-7526

Grand Slam USA
Lancaster Pike/Route 29
Malvern, PA 19355
(610) 647-6622

US Golf
7900 City Line Avenue
Philadelphia, PA 19151
(215) 879-3536

Biking

American Youth Hostels
Philadelphia, PA
(215) 925-6004

Bicycle Coalition
Philadelphia, PA
(215) BICYCLE

Bicycle Club of Philadelphia
Philadelphia, PA
(215) 735-2453

Cycling Enthusiasts of the Delaware Valley
Philadelphia, PA
(215) 338-9159

South Jersey Wheelmen
Vineland, NJ
(609) 327-1336

Bowling

Check your local yellow pages for the lanes nearest you. This is a great family activity!

Canoeing/Tubing/Rafting

Canoes are available at all sites; rentals are by the half day or full day. Inner tubes available where marked (*). (Also see Kayaking, page 144.)

Brandywine River
*Northbrook Canoe, West Chester, PA (610) 793-2279

Delaware River
*Bucks County River Country, Point Pleasant, PA (215) 297-5000
*Wilderness Canoe Trips, Wilmington, DE (302) 654-2227

Lehigh River
Lehigh Rafting Rentals, White Haven, PA (570) 443-4441

New Jersey Pine Barrens
*Bel Haven Lake, Egg Harbor (609) 965-2827
Mick's Canoe Rental, Chatsworth (609) 726-1380
Paradise Lakes Campground, Hammonton
*   (609) 561-7095*
Pine Barrens Canoe Rental,
*   Chatsworth (609) 726-1515*
Wading Pines Campgrounds,
*   Chatsworth (609) 726-1313*

Golf

Young children often prefer miniature golf and putting courses. These places offer miniature golf, putting and driving ranges; some Grand Slam USAs also offer miniature golf. See Baseball, page 140. Check your local phone directory for others.

MINIATURE GOLF

Burholme Golf
401 West Cottman Avenue
Philadelphia, PA 19111
(215) 742-2380

Caln Mini Golf
Downingtown, PA
(610) 269-7040

Family Fun Spot
142A Conchester Highway
Aston, PA 19014
(610) 485-1024

Putt Putt Golf Course
5300 West Baltimore Pike
Clifton Heights, PA 19018
(610) 626-5766

US Golf
7900 City Line Avenue
Philadelphia, PA 19187
(215) 879-3536

PUBLIC COURSES

Byrne Golf Course
9500 Leon Street
Philadelphia, PA 19114
(215) 632-8666

Cobbs Creek Golf Course
78th and Lansdowne Streets
Philadelphia, PA 19151
(215) 877-8707

Juniata Golf Course
N and Cayuga Streets
Philadelphia, PA 19124
(215) 743-4060

Roosevelt Golf Course
2000 Pattison Avenue
Philadelphia, PA 19145
(215) 462-8997

Walnut Lane Golf Course
Walnut Lane and Magdalena
Street
Philadelphia, PA 19128
(215) 482-3370

Hiking

Appalachian Mountain Club (215) 481-0870

Batona Hiking Club (215) 659-3921

Sierra Club, Southeastern Pennsylvania Group (215) 592-4063 or (215) 592-4073

Valley Forge Hiking Club (610) 544-4217

Wilmington Trail Club (302) 654-6577

Horseback Riding

Pony rides and elephant rides are also available at the Philadelphia Zoo.

Ashford Farms, Inc.
Box 52, River Road
Miquon, PA 19452
(215) 825-9838

Sheeder Mill Farm
Sheeder Mill & Pughtown Roads
Sheeder, PA 19460
(610) 469-9382

Gateway Stables
949 Merrybell Lane
Kennett Square, PA 19348
(610) 444-9928

Ice Skating

These rinks are open to the public. Call for hours.

Class of 1923 Rink
University of Pennsylvania
3130 Walnut Street
Philadelphia, PA 19104
(215) 898-1923

Coliseum
333 Preston Avenue
Voorhees, NJ 08043
(609) 216-0003

Evesham Skating Center
Evesboro-Medford Road
Marlton, NJ 08053
(609) 983-3500

Face-Off Circle
1185 Old York Road
Warminster, PA 18974
(215) 674-1345

General Washington Recreation Center
2750 Egypt Road
Audubon, PA 19407
(610) 666-7603

Old York Road Skating Club
Church Road
Elkins Park, PA 19117
(215) 635-0331

RiverRink at Penn's Landing
Columbus Boulevard
* at Chestnut Street*
Philadelphia, PA 19106
(215) 629-3200
(215) 925-RINK (recording)

Rizzo Rink
Front and Washington Streets
Philadelphia, PA 19047
(215) 685-1593

(*continued on next page*)

Simon's
Walnut Lane and Woolfton Street
Philadelphia, PA 19138
(215) 685-2888

Skating Club of Wilmington
1303 Carruthers Lane
Wilmington, DE 19803
(302) 656-5005

Skatium
Darby and Manoa Roads
Havertown, PA 19083
(610) 853-2225/2226

Viking Ice Arena
431 Valley Forge Road
King of Prussia, PA 19406
(610) 354-9282

Warwick Twin Rinks
1621 Mearns Road
Warwick, PA 18974
(215) 441-5184

Winter Sport Ice Arena
York Road
Willow Grove, PA 19090
(215) 659-4253

Wissahickon Skating Club
550 Willow Grove Avenue
   and Cherokee Road
Chestnut Hill, PA 19118
(215) 247-1907

Kayaking

Island Kayaks
116 Stone Harbor Boulevard
Stone Harbor, NJ 08247
(609) 368-1001

TI Kayaks
5006 Landis Avenue
Sea Isle City, NJ 08243
(609) 263-0805

League Sports

Little League baseball, softball, football, soccer, and other sports flourish throughout the area. Contact your township Recreation Director or Civic Association for information. The Challenger Softball program for mentally and physically handicapped children operates under official Little League auspices (717-326-1921).

Rock Climbing

Philadelphia Rock Gym
422 Business Center
East 520 North Circle Drive
Oaks, PA 19456
(610) 666-ROPE

Vertical Extreme
462 Acorn Lane
Downingtown, PA 19335
(610) 873-9620

Vertical Reality
67 Old King's Highway
Maple Shade, NJ 08052
(609) 273-1370

Roller Skating

CN Skate Palace, Ltd.
247 Concord Road
Aston, PA 19014
(610) 494-4443

Carman Gardens Roller Skating Rink
3226 Germantown Avenue
Philadelphia, PA 19133
(215) 223-2200

Cherry Hill Skating Center
661 Old Cuthbert and Deer Roads
Cherry Hill, NJ 08034
(609) 795-1919

Cornwells Roller Skating Center
2350 Bristol Pike
Cornwells Heights, PA 19020
(215) 638-7766

Deptford Skating Center
Cedar and Deptford Avenues
Westville, NJ 08093
(609) 845-7353/2490

Echelon Skating Center
1140 White Horse Road
Voorhees, NJ 08043
(609) 346-1335

Elmwood Roller Skating Rink
2406 South 71st Street
Philadelphia, PA 19142
(215) 492-8543

Embassy Roller Skating Center
2229 East Buck Road
Pennsburg, PA 18073
(215) 679-3800

Evesham Skating Center
Evesboro-Medford Road
Marlton, NJ 08053
(609) 983-3500

Franklin Skating Center
Delsea Drive
Franklinville, NJ 08322
(609) 694-0600

Holiday Roller Skating Center
Creek Road
Delanco, NJ 08075
(609) 461-3770

Palace Roller Skating Center
11586 Roosevelt Boulevard
Philadelphia, PA 19154
(215) 698-8000

Rollerama Skating Center
Route 413 and New Falls Road
Levittown, PA 19059
(215) 949-2782

Villanova Skating Arena
Lancaster Avenue
Villanova, PA 19085
(610) 527-7465

Skiing: Cross Country

Camp Speers
Dingman's Ferry, PA 18328
(570) 828-2329

Crystal Lake Ski Area
Hughesville, PA 17737
(570) 584-2698

Hanley's Happy Hill
Eagles Mere, PA 17731
(570) 525-3461

Jack Frost
White Haven, PA 18661
(570) 443-8425

Ridley Creek State Park
Media, PA 19063
(610) 892-3900

Skiing: Downhill/Snowboarding/Tubing

Most of the skiing mountains listed below have tubing and
allow snowboarding. Call to confirm before heading out. (Call
1-800-POCONOS for ski conditions.)

Alpine Mountain
Analomink, PA 18320
(570) 595-2150

Belle Mountain
Lambertville, NJ 08530
(609) 397-0043

Big Boulder
Blakeslee, PA 18610
(570) 722-0101

Blue Mountain Ski Area
Palmerton, PA 18071
(610) 826-7700

Camelback Mountain
Tannersville, PA 18372
(570) 629-1661

Doe Mountain
Macungie, PA 18062
(610) 682-7109

Elk Mountain
Union Dale, PA 18470
(570) 679-2611

Heidelberg Ski Area
Route 183 and Robesonia Road
Bernville, PA 19506
(610) 488-6399

Jack Frost
White Haven, PA 18661
(570) 443-8425

Montage
Scranton, PA 18805
(570) 969-7669

Shawnee
Shawnee-on-Delaware, PA 18356
(570) 421-7231

Ski Liberty Ski Resort
78 Country Club Trail
Carroll Valley, PA 17320
(717) 642-8282

Ski Roundtop
925 Roundtop Road
Lewisberry, PA 17339
(717) 432-9631

Split Rock
Lake Harmony, PA 18624
(570) 722-9111

Spring Mountain Ski Area
Schwenksville, PA 19473
(610) 287-7900

Tanglewood Ski Area
Route 390
Tafton, PA 18464
(570) 226-7669

Tennis

Many neighborhood parks have public courts. Call your township Recreation Department for information.

Arthur Ashe Youth Tennis Center
(indoors, October-April)

4015 Main Street
Philadelphia, PA 19127
(215) 487-9555

Spectator Sports

The Philadelphia area sizzles with colorful teams and emotional fans. The hot teams are listed below, but until hero-worship and team loyalties become a factor, consider taking a young child to a farm league or college game where the crowds aren't overwhelming and the child can sit close to the action. Farm league and pro information is listed with each sport.

Baseball
Philadelphia Phillies
Veterans Stadium (215) 463-1000

Reading Phillies
(610) 375-8469

Scranton Red Barons
(570) 969-2255

Basketball
Philadelphia 76ers
First Union Complex (215) 336-3600

Football
Philadelphia Eagles
Veterans Stadium (215) 463-5500

Scranton Eagles
(570) 969-2255

Hockey
AHL Ice Hockey:
Philadelphia Phantoms
First Union Complex (215) 336-3600

NHL Ice Hockey:
Philadelphia Flyers
First Union Complex (215) 336-3600

Indoor Lacrosse
Philadelphia Wings
First Union Complex (215) 336-3600

Indoor Soccer
KiXX
First Union Complex (215) 336-3600

Rodeo
Cowtown Rodeo
Route 40
Woodstown, NJ 08098
(609) 769-3200/3207

Hours: Memorial Day to end of September: Saturday, 7:30 PM.

Unique Areas

Bridgeton, New Jersey, is the state's largest historic district with 2200 registered National Historic sites!

Germantown is a section of Philadelphia known for its historic buildings, as the site of an important Revolutionary War battle, and as the location of stations on the Underground Railroad that brought slaves to freedom in the North.

Hershey, Pennsylvania, is a fine example of a caring company helping to develop resources within a town for everyone's benefit.

Lancaster, Pennsylvania, is famous for the kind hospitality offered by members of its Amish, Mennonite and Hutterite communities. Magnificent countryside provides a scenic background for farms open to the public and numerous railroad and farm life museums that children love.

Bridgeton, New Jersey

Driving: From Philadelphia, take the Ben Franklin or Walt Whitman Bridge to I-676 South. Follow I-676 to Route 130 South to Route 45 South to Route 77 South. Continue along Route 77 South into the town of Bridgeton. Go left on West Commerce Street, then left onto Aitken Drive. Individual directions for highlights follow.

Tours/Programs: The Bridgeton-Cumberland Tourist Association (Routes 77 and 49) offers bus and trolley tours and cassette tapes for walking tours of historic Bridgeton, (609) 451-4802.

Cohanzick Zoo

City of Bridgeton Park
Bridgeton, NJ 08302
(609) 455-3230 (City Hall), ext. 242

Hours: Daily 9 AM-5 PM.

Cost: Free.

Description: Small zoo features birds and small primates. Local animals include fox, raccoon and skunk. Large mammals range from black bear and mountain lion to zebra.

Time Needed: 30 minutes.

Eating: OK in Park, not in Zoo.

Driving: When you enter Bridgeton on Route 77 South, turn right at the light onto Washington Street. At dead end, go right, enter Park and watch for signs.

Hall of Fame Sports Museum

Babe Ruth Drive and Burt Street
Bridgeton, NJ 08302
(609) 451-7300

Hours: Tuesday-Saturday, 10 AM-12 noon and 1 PM-3 PM.

Cost: Free.

Description: Extensive collection of local and national sports memorabilia. Trophy Room has famous cups and awards from baseball, boxing, football, and the Olympics. Photos, uniforms, bats and balls from local teams, the Philadelphia Phillies, and the Cincinnati Reds. Don't miss Willie Mays' Golden Glove.

(*continued on next page*)

Driving: From Bridgeton's Aitken Drive, follow signs for the Recreation Center. Take the first left onto Babe Ruth Drive, Museum is at the next corner (Babe Ruth Drive and Burt Street).

Nail House Museum

1 Aitken Drive
Bridgeton, NJ 08302
(609) 455-4100

Hours: April-December: Tuesday-Friday, 10 AM-3:30 PM; Saturday-Sunday, 11 AM-4 PM.

Cost: Free, donations appreciated.

Description: 19th-century men and boys labored here to make iron nails used throughout the United States. Tools of the trade and an old water-powered nail machine on display. Check the Nail Master's desk and its secret drawer lined with the original newspaper announcing Lincoln's death.

Time Needed: 30 minutes.

Driving: Museum is immediately to your right as you turn onto Aitken Drive from West Commerce Street.

Sweden Farmstead Museum

(609) 455-9785

Hours: May-September: Sunday and holidays, 12 noon-5 PM; Summer: Wednesday-Friday, 11 AM-5 PM.

Cost: $3.00 adults, $2.50 seniors, $2.00 students, $1.50 under 12, under 6 free.

Description: Recreation of one of Bridgeton's earliest Swedish villages. Seven buildings include a farmhouse, smokehouse, and barn. Costumed guides tell all about life in the original settlement.

Woodruff Indian Museum

Bridgeton Free Public Library
East Commerce Street
Bridgeton, NJ 08302
(609) 451-2620

Hours: Monday-Friday, 2 PM-4 PM; Saturday, 1 PM-3 PM.

Cost: Free.

Description: More than 2000 artifacts have been donated to the museum, including arrowheads, pieces of clay pots, beads, smoking pipes, and other items used by the Nanicoke Lenni-Lenape Indians native to the area.

Time Needed: 45 minutes.

Driving: Follow Route 77 South to Bridgeton, then turn right onto East Commerce Street.

Germantown, Philadelphia

Driving: With a street map of Philadelphia in your pocket, take I-76 (Schuylkill Expressway) West to the Lincoln Drive exit. Follow Lincoln Drive until it dead-ends at Allen's Lane. Turn right to Germantown Avenue. From here, your street map will be useful.

Awbury Arboretum

Chew Avenue and Washington Lane
Philadelphia, PA 19144
(215) 849-2855 (City Parks Association)

Hours: Dawn to dusk.

Cost: Free.

Description: 57 acres in Germantown provide ample space to appreciate nature and the legacy of the Cope family. One 250-year-old black oak tree is older than our country. Please note that some of the houses are private residences and not open to the public.

Cliveden

6401 Germantown Avenue
Philadelphia, PA 19144
(215) 848-1777

Hours: April-December: Thursday-Sunday, 12 noon-4 PM.

Cost: $6.00 adults, $4.00 children and students.

Description: Elegant furniture and memorabilia from more than 200 years of Chew family history have been kept in this historic house museum. Young visitors enjoy the family's treasures and trivia along with the scars left on the building from the Battle of Germantown on October 4, 1777.

Tours/Programs: Tours on the hour, good programs for school groups.

Eating: Indoor and outdoor picnic facilities.

Concord Schoolhouse

6313 Germantown Avenue
Philadelphia, PA 19144

Cost: $2.50 adults, $1.50 children.

Description: One-room schoolhouse in the corner of Germantown's Upper Burying Ground. Records and trustee meeting minutes have been kept since 1776. Original furniture, lanterns, desks, and books reflect the sparse simplicity of this strict schoolroom, where learning was a privilege and unruly students were not allowed to attend. Visits by appointment only, call (215) 843-0943.

Cunningham Piano Company

See Working World, page 174.

Deshler-Morris House

5442 Germantown Avenue
Philadelphia, PA 19144
(215) 596-1748

Hours: April-December: Tuesday-Saturday, 1 PM-4 PM.

Cost: $1.00 adults, $.50 children.

Description: Known as the "Germantown White House" because George Washington lived here from 1793 to 1794 to escape the yellow fever plaguing Philadelphia. (At that time, Philadelphia was the capital of the country.) The President's bedroom is on the second floor front.

Ebenezer Maxwell Mansion

200 West Tulpehocken Street
Philadelphia, PA 19144
(215) 438-1861   ⊤ 🚌

Hours: April-December: Friday-Sunday, 1 PM-4 PM.

Cost: $4.00 adults, $2.00 children, $3.00 seniors.

Description: Wonderful Victorian architecture and use of wrought iron. Guided tours tell about the roles of parents, children, and servants in the mid-19th century. Children may try out antique toys and household items.

Tours/Programs: Very good programs encourage children to compare family lifestyles as well as neighboring architectural styles. Role-playing opportunities for school groups.

Germantown Historical Society Museum

5501-05 Germantown Avenue
Philadelphia, PA 19144
(215) 844-0514/1683   ♿ *(museum only)* ☂

Hours: Tuesday and Thursday, 10 AM-4 PM; Sunday, 1 PM-5 PM. Closed major holidays.

Cost: Museum: $4.00 per person; Library: $7.50.

Description: Changing exhibits depict the early history of "German Township," in the northwest section of Philadelphia. Toys, costumes, decorative arts, and battle paraphernalia appeal to children.

Tours/Programs: 1-hour tour (no wandering alone).

Eating: Picnics possible on the lawn.

Germantown Mennonite Historic Trust

6117 Germantown Avenue
Philadelphia, PA 19144
(215) 843-0943   ☂ 🚌

Hours: By appointment only.

Cost: $3.00 adults, $1.50 children.

Description: Site of the first Mennonite church in the colonies. First recorded protest against slavery signed here in 1688. See Johnson House (page 158).

Grumblethorpe

5267 Germantown Avenue
Philadelphia, PA 19144
(215) 843-4820   ☂ 🚌

Hours: Tuesday, Thursday, Sunday, 1 PM-4 PM.

Cost: $3.00 adults, $1.50 children.

Description: Furnished house and garden, built in 1744.

Historic RittenhouseTown

See History, page 20.

Johnson House

6306 Germantown Avenue
Philadelphia, PA 19144
(215) 438-1768

Hours: Thursday-Saturday, 1 PM-4 PM, or by appointment.

Cost: $3.00 adults, $1.50 children.

Description: 18th-century Mennonite house and garden. Germantown was a stop along the Underground Railroad that helped slaves fleeing from bondage. Quaker and Mennonite religious beliefs "knew slavery to be a sin against God" and aided fugitive slaves in their flight to freedom.

Paley Design Center

Philadelphia College of Textiles and Science
4200 Henry Avenue
Philadelphia, PA 19144
(215) 951-2860

Hours: Tuesday-Friday, 10 AM-4 PM; Saturday-Sunday, 12 noon-4 PM.

Cost: Free.

Description: Ethnic costumes, children's clothes nearly 100 years old, collections of feathers, fabrics, shoes, shells, and hundreds of colorful designs. Most in storage and can be retrieved by appointment for interested students. Exhibit Hall open to the public.

Stenton

18th and Windrim Streets
Philadelphia, PA 19144
(215) 329-7312

Hours: March-December: Thursday-Saturday, 1 PM-4 PM; Tuesday and Wednesday by appointment.

Cost: $5.00 adults, $4.00 students and seniors, under 6 free.

Description: George Washington used this building as his headquarters, but children are usually more interested in the restored barn, orangery, and weaving shed.

Upsala

6430 Germantown Avenue
Philadelphia, PA 19144
(215) 842-1798/438-4775

Hours: Thursday and Saturday, 1 PM-4 PM.

Cost: $5.00 adults, $2.00 children.

Description: Washington's soldiers placed their cannons on Upsala's lawns to blast the British occupying Cliveden across the street.

Woodmere Art Museum

9201 Germantown Avenue
Philadelphia, PA 19118
(215) 247-0476

Hours: Tuesday-Saturday, 10 AM-5 PM; Sunday, 1 PM-5 PM. Closed Mondays and holidays.

Cost: Recommended donations: $5.00 adults, $3.00 seniors, $2.00 students, under 12 free.

Description: Museum collection blends historical and cultural artifacts. Children's Gallery has work done by children for other children to view. Many arts classes for children and adults throughout the year.

Time Needed: 30 minutes.

Wyck

6026 Germantown Avenue
Philadelphia, PA 19144
(215) 848-1690

Hours: April-December: Tuesday, Thursday, and Saturday, 1 PM-4 PM. By appointment year-round, Tuesday-Saturday, 9 AM-4 PM.

Cost: $5.00 adults, $4.00 students and seniors, $10.00 family.

Description: Oldest family home in Germantown, built in 1689. Personal toys, treasures, and architectural genius make this house come to life for visitors.

Hershey, Pennsylvania
"Chocolate Town, U.S.A."

Hershey, PA 17033
(717) 534-3005, or 1-800-533-3131
www.hersheypa.com   ♿ ⛪ 🚐 🎂 *(all attractions)*

Individual costs are listed under each attraction. To reach any exhibit, it's best to follow directions to main parking lot, then take the appropriate tram to each attraction. Reach Zoo by car; no tram from parking lot.

Accommodations include hotels, motels, and campgrounds. All Hershey facilities closed on Thanksgiving, Christmas, New Year's Day, and Easter Sunday.

Eating: Best in Park and Chocolate World. Picnic tables scattered throughout, covered tables near parking lot.

Driving: Take PA Turnpike West to exit 20 (Lebanon-Lancaster). Follow Route 72 North to Route 322 West to Hershey.

Chocolate World

Hershey, PA 17033
(717) 534-4900

Hours: Times vary—call ahead.

Cost: Free.

Description: Visitors sit in vehicles that wind through a lively exhibit telling the story of chocolate—from beans in tropical forests to candy bars and cocoa. It's hard to resist the huge sundaes at the Dessert Cafe!

Founders Hall

At the Milton Hershey School
Hershey, PA 17033
(717) 520-2000

Hours: January-March: daily 10 AM-3 PM; April-December: daily 10 AM-4 PM. Closed Easter, Thanksgiving, and Christmas.

Cost: Free.

Description: Displays include memorabilia from the Milton Hershey School and, in the Giant Rotunda, a film called *The Vision*.

Hershey Gardens

Hershey, PA 17033
(717) 534-3492

Hours: April-Memorial Day: daily 9 AM-5 PM; Memorial Day-Labor Day: Monday-Thursday, 9 AM-6 PM, Friday-Sunday, 9 AM-8 PM; Labor Day-October: daily 9 AM-5 PM. Closed November-March. Butterfly House: mid-June-mid-September: daily 9 AM-6 PM (closed for inclement weather).

Cost: $6.00 adults, $3.00 children 3-15, under 3 free.

Description: 23 acres of colorful, fragrant flowers, shrubs, and trees. Massed plantings of 50,000 tulips in April, 14,000 roses in June, and 13,000 annuals all summer are just three of the impressive displays. New butterfly house with 400 to 500 butterflies, all native American species.

Hershey Museum

Hershey, PA 17033
(717) 534-3439

Hours: Memorial Day-Labor Day: daily 9 AM-6 PM; Labor Day-Memorial Day: daily 10 AM-5 PM.

Cost: $6.00 adults, $3.00 children 3-15, under 3 free.

Description: Learn about the town built on chocolate. See Milton Hershey's Native American and Pennsylvania German collections. Hands-on discovery room for kids.

HersheyPark

Hershey, PA 17033
(717) 534-3900, 1-800-HERSHEY

Hours: May-August and September weekends: opens 10 AM daily, closing time varies between 6 PM and 11 PM.

Cost: $30.95 ages 9-54, $16.95 seniors and children 3-8.

Description: 65 exciting rides and attractions for all ages. With seven roller coasters, they now have more than any other park in Pennsylvania. If you plan on going on the big rides, get to those early as the lines can get very long.

HersheyPark Christmas Candyland

Description: At the entrance to HersheyPark, from mid-November through December. More than half a million lights with rides, shops, and entertainment.

Zoo America

North American Wildlife Park
Hershey, PA 17033
(717) 534-3860

Hours: Daily 10 AM, various closing times.

Cost: $5.75 adults, $5.25 seniors, $4.50 children 3-12, under 3 free. (If you're going to HersheyPark also, go there first as your park admission fee also includes admission to the Zoo.)

Description: Animals and plants from five regions of North America. Alligators, black bears, elk, and bison. More than 200 animals in attractive, 11-acre park setting.

Lancaster, Pennsylvania

Children of the Nintendo Nineties find a very different lifestyle in this gentle, rolling farm country: no TV, no video games, often no electricity. One-room schoolhouses, distinct black carriages in place of cars, and respect for each other reflect the Amish, Mennonite, and Hutterite beliefs. See Horse-drawn Carriage Tours, page 138.

Driving: From Philadelphia, go west on Route 30. Or take PA Turnpike west to exit 23 (Downington), then south on Route 100 and west on Route 30. The majority of attractions listed are along Route 30 *before* the city of Lancaster. See Lancaster map, page 215.

Pennsylvania Dutch Visitors Bureau

501 Greenfield Road
Lancaster, PA 17601
(717) 299-8901

Hours: May-August: Monday-Saturday, 8 AM-6 PM; Sunday, 8 AM-5 PM; September-October: Sunday-Thursday, 8:30 AM-5 PM; Friday-Saturday, 8:30 AM-6 PM; November-April: daily 9 AM-5 PM.

Cost: Free.

Description: Information on all Lancaster places and events. A 15-minute film, *People, Places, and Passions*, explains the history and heritage of the area and its people. Free map and visitors guide available.

Amish Country Homestead

Amish Experience Theater
Route 340
Bird-in-Hand, PA 17505
(717) 768-3600 or (800) 441-3505

Hours: Theater: Monday-Saturday, 9 AM-8 PM; Sunday, 11 AM-6 PM; Homestead: Monday-Saturday, 9 AM-7 PM; Sunday, 11 AM-5 PM. Bus tour: May-November: Monday-Saturday, 10:30 AM, 2 PM; Sunday, 11:30 AM. December-April: Saturday and Sunday only, 11:30 AM.

Cost: Theater: $6.50 adults, $3.75 children ages 4-12, under 4 free. House tour: $5.00 adults, $3.25 children 4-12, under 4 free. Bus tour: $18.95 adults, $10.95 children.

(*continued on next page*)

Description: Learn about the Old-Order Amish in the 35-minute theater presentation of "Jacob's Choice." Tour through the Country Homestead and watch the children discover life without electricity! The 2-hour and 15-minute guided bus tour takes you through the surrounding farmland.

Eating: Family-style restaurant.

Amish Farm and House

2395 Lincoln Highway East (Route 30)
Lancaster, PA 17602
(717) 394-6185

Hours: November-May: daily 8:30 AM-4 PM; September-October: daily 8:30 AM-5 PM; June, July, August: daily 8:30 AM-6 PM.

Cost: $5.95 adults, $5.50 seniors, $3.50 children 5-11, under 5 free.

Description: Farm has everything from hatching eggs to tobacco crops. The house is filled with curiosities, from Indian artifacts to children's toys. Brave children love to climb in and out of the casket in the bedroom. Foreign language tours available.

Eating: Covered picnic areas, Dutch food pavilion.

Amish Village

Route 896, P.O. Box 115
Strasburg, PA 17579
(717) 687-8511

Hours: January-mid-March (house only): Saturday-Sunday, 10 AM-4 PM; mid-March-November: daily 9 AM-5 PM; December (house only): daily 10 AM-4 PM. Closing times may vary so call ahead if you plan on going late.

Cost: House only: $3.00 adults, $1.50 children 6-12, under 6 free. House and grounds: $5.75 adults, $2.00 children 6-12, under 6 free.

Description: Guided house tour takes 30 minutes, but more time is needed to see blacksmith shop, operating smokehouse and water wheel, farm animals and one-room schoolhouse.

Anderson Bakery

2060 Old Philadelphia Pike (Route 340)
Lancaster, PA 17602
(717) 299-2321

Hours: Monday-Friday, 8:30 AM-4 PM.

Cost: Free.

Description: Walk along the glass-enclosed catwalk above a fully automated pretzel factory. Twenty-minute, self-guided tour shows dough being mixed, formed into pretzels, baked, and packaged.

Candy Americana Museum/ Wilbur Chocolates

46 North Broad Street
Lititz, PA 17543
(717) 626-1131

Hours: Monday-Saturday, 10 AM-5 PM.

Cost: Free.

Description: Exhibit shows how candy was made by hand in the past and displays many candy molds in different shapes.

Choo-Choo Barn

Route 741 East, Box 130
Strasburg, PA 17579
(717) 687-7911

Hours: April-December: 10 AM-5 PM. Closed January-March.

Cost: $4.00 over age 12, $2.00 children 4-12, under 4 free.

Description: Giant layout of O-gauge model trains running through and around villages and mountains. Real waterfalls, a circus, fire engines putting out a house on fire, a total of 125 animated objects. Day and night scenes.

> Pennsylvania's nicknames are the Quaker State and the Keystone State.

Discover Lancaster County History Museum

Route 30
Lancaster, PA 17602
(717) 393-3679   ♿ ⬆ 🚌

Hours: Memorial Day-Labor Day: daily 9 AM-9 PM; Labor Day-Memorial Day: daily 9 AM-5 PM.

Cost: $5.95 adults, $5.50 seniors, $3.50 children 5-11, under 5 free.

Description: Lifelike scenes with good graphics explain the history of Lancaster County. One scene depicts the day (September 27, 1777) when Lancaster was capital of the United States! Watch for Ben Franklin, Abe Lincoln, George Washington, Daniel Boone. Simulated barn-raising near end of tour is especially fun. Look for tired workman near Davy Crockett. Younger children will also have fun with the hands-on exhibits.

Tours/Programs: Audio tour available.

Dutch Wonderland

2249 Route 30 East
Lancaster, PA 17602
(717) 291-1888   ♿ 🚌 🎂

Hours: Mid-April through May: Saturday, 10 AM-6 PM; Sunday, 11 AM-6 PM; Memorial Day weekend-Labor Day: Monday-Saturday, 10 AM-7 PM; Labor Day-mid-October: Saturday, 10 AM-6 PM; Sunday, 11 AM-6 PM.

Cost: $12.00, admission and five rides; $17.00, admission and unlimited rides; under 2 free.

Description: Perfect amusement park for younger children. Boats, cars, trains, double-splash roller coaster, high dive demonstration, family parachute ride, and animated show. Monorail around the park (additional charge).

Eating: Concession stands, cafeteria, restaurant.

Eagle Falls

See Amusement Parks, page 125.

Ephrata Cloister

632 West Main Street
Ephrata, PA 17522
(717) 733-6600

Hours: Monday-Saturday, 9 AM-5 PM; Sunday, 12 noon-5 PM.

Cost: $6.00 adults, $5.50 seniors, $4.00 ages 6-12, under 6 free.

Description: One of America's earliest religious societies began here in 1732. They built medieval-style buildings and lived a life of self-denial and discipline. Their important paper industry (books and broadside printing) has been famous since 1743 for its beautiful calligraphy and illuminated work. Examples of their handcrafted furniture, basket making, and unusual music are everywhere. Children are amazed at how tiny the residents' bedrooms were.

Time Needed: 1 1/2 hours.

Tours/Programs: Do not miss 40-minute tour of main building. Vorspiel, a musical drama depicting cloister life and featuring cloister music, is presented weekend evenings from July to September.

Eating: Picnics allowed.

Folk Craft Center and Museum

Mount Sidney Road
Witmer, PA 17585
www.folkcraftcenter.com

Hours: March-November: Monday-Saturday, 9:30 AM-5 PM; Sunday, 12 noon-4 PM. December-February: by appointment only.

Cost: $5.00 adults, $4.00 seniors, $3.00 children 6-16, under 6 free, $12.00 family rate.

Description: Professional slide show spans the different seasons and lifestyles of the Pennsylvania Dutch. Museum gallery has exhibits on Pennsylvania Dutch folklore, barn-raising, and "Meet the Mennonites." Great Hall is a replica of a Mennonite house, including walk-in fireplace. In the back, look for herb garden, woodworker's shed, and 1762 Weave Haus with old beam loom still in use.

Time Needed: 1 hour.

Tours/Programs: 15-minute slide presentation, "The Land We Love."

Hands-on House

2380 Kissel Hill Road
Lancaster, PA 17601
(717) 569-KIDS

Hours: Winter: Tuesday-Thursday, 11 AM-4 PM; Friday, 11 AM-8 PM; Saturday, 10 AM-5 PM; Sunday, 12 noon-5 PM; closed Mondays and major holidays. Memorial Day-Labor Day: Monday-Thursday, 10 AM-5 PM; Friday, 10 AM-8 PM; Saturday, 10 AM-5 PM; Sunday, 12 noon-5 PM.

Cost: $4.00 per person.

Description: This converted Victorian house offers plenty for 2- to 10-year-old visitors and their parents. Changing exhibit rooms include Corner Grocery, Once Upon a Forest, Face-to-Face, Under Construction, I Spy, Switch on Art, and Space Voyage Checkpoint.

Driving: Route 30 West to Route 272 North. Go left on Landis Valley Road. The Museum is the first house on the left, opposite the Pennsylvania Farm Museum.

Hans Herr House

Hans Herr Drive
Lancaster, PA 17602
(717) 464-4438

Hours: April-November: Monday-Saturday, 9 AM-4 PM. Last tour at 3:30 PM.

Cost: $3.50 adults, $1.00 children 7-12, under 7 free.

Description: Oldest house in Lancaster County (1719); oldest Mennonite church in North America. Step into the fireplace and look up the chimney; see where the children slept in the attic. Outside, look for a full range of farming implements, blacksmith shop, bake oven, smokehouse, and apple orchards. Try your hand at pumping water from the original well.

Eating: Picnic tables.

There are 4,500 rivers and streams in Pennsylvania, and over 300 lakes.

Kitchen Kettle Village

Route 340
Intercourse, PA 17534
(717) 768-8261

Hours: Monday-Saturday, 9 AM-5 PM. Closed major holidays.

Description: Twenty shops offer local crafts and home-baked treats. Jellies and relishes, baked goods, crafts, and candy made right there.

Lancaster Newspaper Newseum

South Queen Street
Lancaster, PA 17601
(717) 291-8600 (Lancaster Newspapers, Inc.)

Glass-enclosed exhibit on street showing old printing presses with captions explaining use of machines.

Mennonite Heritage Center

The Meeting House
565 Yoder Road
Harleysville, PA 19438
(215) 256-3020　　　　　　　　 ♿ ⛺ 🚐

Hours: Tuesday-Friday, 10 AM-5 PM; Saturday, 10 AM-2 PM; Sunday, 2 PM-5 PM.

Cost: Free.

Description: Three centuries of Anabaptist-Mennonite heritage. Strong emphasis on family. Special programs for school groups. Library, museum, and shop.

Mill Bridge Village and Campground

Box 86, Ronks Road
Strasburg, PA 17579
(717) 687-8181

Hours: April-October: daily 9:30 AM-5:30 PM; November: Saturday-Sunday, 9:30 AM-5 PM.

Cost: $10.00 adults, $8.00 seniors, $5.00 children 6-12, under 6 free.

Description: Free Amish buggy rides with paid admission. Visit the 1738 Mill, still operating, with an exhibit upstairs. In the village, watch broom makers at work, visit shops and craftspeople. Campground welcomes all campers, tents to RVs, and has old-fashioned playground for children.

North Museum of Franklin and Marshall College

College and Buchanan Streets
P.O. Box 3003
Lancaster, PA 17604
(717) 291-3941

Hours: Tuesday-Saturday, 9 AM-5 PM; Sunday, 12 noon-5 PM. Closed major holidays.

Cost: $2.00 per person; under 4 free. Planetarium show: $1.50 per person at 1 PM, $2.50 per person at 2 PM and 3 PM.

Description: Small natural history museum with collections of skeletons, Indian artifacts, animals, and a large rock and mineral display. Visit the Discovery Room for hands-on experiences and the Live Animal Room. Planetarium shows Saturday and Sunday at 1 PM (especially directed toward younger viewers and families), 2 PM, and 3 PM.

Time Needed: 2 hours.

Tours/Programs: Many special programs throughout the year.

Pennsylvania Farm Museum of Landis Valley

2451 Kissel Hill Road
Lancaster, PA 17601
(717) 569-0401

Hours: Monday-Saturday, 9 AM-5 PM; Sunday, 12 noon-5 PM. Closed major holidays. Last tour at 3:30 PM.

Cost: $7.00 adults, $5.00 children 6-12, $6.50 seniors, under 6 free, $19.00 family.

Description: Fantastic collection of buildings with 22 exhibit areas put together to demonstrate the traditional way of life in rural Pennsylvania. Tour goes through some buildings, others you explore on your own. See old wagons, fire-fighting equipment, tin and pottery shops, country store-as-it-was, and many farming tools. Two farmsteads with animals and costumed interpreters give life to the site.

Time Needed: Minimum 1 hour.

Tours/Programs: 1-hour guided tour.

Eating: Picnic areas. Inn restaurant open May-October.

People's Place

Route 340
Intercourse, PA 17534
(717) 768-7171

Hours: April-Labor Day: Monday-Saturday, 9:30 AM-8 PM; Labor Day-March: Monday-Saturday, 9:30 AM-5 PM.

Cost: For one attraction: $4.00 adults, $2.00 children; for both attractions: $7.00 adults, $3.50 children.

Description: One attraction is "Twenty Questions," a hands-on museum for children including the Feeling Box, barn-raising book, energy quiz, and dress-up room. The other attraction is the 30-minute film, *Who are the Amish?*

Railroad Museum of Pennsylvania

Route 741, Box 15
Strasburg, PA 17579
(717) 687-8628

Hours: Tuesday-Saturday, 9 AM-5 PM; Sunday, 12 noon-5 PM.

Cost: $6.00 adults, $4.00 children 6-17, under 6 free, $5.50 seniors, $16.00 family.

(*continued on next page*)

Description: Nearly 100 historic locomotives and railcars. Brave visitors can walk under a 62-ton steam locomotive. Tremendous collection of glorious old rail cars (Pullman cars and private stateroom cars included) along with railroad memorabilia from conductors' hats to fancy dining china. Combine with a trip across the street to ride on the Strasburg railroad. Visit the railway education center.

Time Needed: 1 hour.

Eating: None, but the Strasburg Railroad across the street has a picnic area and restaurant.

Rock Ford Plantation and Kauffman Museum

881 Rock Ford Road
P.O. Box 264
Lancaster, PA 17603
(717) 392-7223

Hours: April-October: Tuesday-Friday, 10 AM-4 PM; Sunday, 12 noon-4 PM. Last tour at 3 PM.

Cost: $5.00 adults, $3.00 children 6-12, $4.00 seniors, under 6 free.

Description: Costumed guides lead good, kid-centered tours of this historic Georgian mansion, once owned by Lancaster's leading physician and Revolutionary war hero. Open-hearth cooking demonstrations and a complimentary, hearth-baked gingersnap cookie are always a big hit for all.

Tours/Programs: Halloween and Christmas candlelight tours.

Eating: Many picnic areas in surrounding park.

Strasburg Railroad

See Train Rides, page 138.

Sturgis Pretzel House

219 East Main Street
Lititz, PA 17543
(717) 626-4354

Hours: Monday-Saturday, 9 AM-5 PM. Last tour at 4:30.

Cost: $2.00 adults.

Description: Allow plenty of time to visit—this is great fun! Hear how the early pretzel makers earned two cents for every 100 pretzels they made, then try twisting the dough yourself. Watch modern machines produce at the rate of 5 tons of pretzels an hour. See soft pretzels being made and then cooked in the original ovens.

Your admission ticket is a pretzel!

Time Needed: 1 hour (including 30-minute tour).

Toy Train Museum

P.O. Box 248
Strasburg, PA 17579
(717) 687-8976

Hours: Daily 10 AM-5 PM. Closed January-March. Weekends only, November-December. Daily Christmas week.

Cost: $3.00 adults, $1.50 children 6-12, under 6 free.

Description: The Train Collectors Association has assembled a collection of toy tinplate trains ranging from the mid-1800s to the present day. Also featured are five interactive operating train layouts and a train video. Movie and collectors' information available.

Watch and Clock Museum of the NAWCC

514 Poplar Street
Columbia, PA 17512
(717) 684-8261

Hours: Tuesday-Saturday, 10 AM-5 PM; Sunday, 12 noon-4 PM.

Cost: $6.00 adults, $4.00 children 6-12, under 6 free, $16.00 family.

Description: Newly renovated museum takes you through a Time Tunnel tracing 3,500 years of timekeeping beginning with Stonehenge. Various thematic and interactive exhibits are of special interest to kids. Introductory video, *Yours, Mine and Hours,* is a good way to start your visit.

Time Needed: 1 hour to 1 1/2 hours.

Weavertown One-Room Schoolhouse

Old Philadelphia Pike (Route 340)
Bird-in-Hand, PA 17505
(717) 768-3976

Hours: April-Labor Day: daily 9 AM-5 PM; Labor Day-October: daily 10 AM-5 PM; March and November: Saturday-Sunday, 10 AM-5 PM; closed December-February.

Cost: $2.95 adults, $2.50 seniors, $1.95 children 5-11, under 5 free.

Description: Life-size animated figures, in a 15-minute show, depict education in a one-room schoolhouse. Real classes took place as recently as 1969; now they're all dummies.

Wheatland

1120 Marietta Avenue (Route 23)
Lancaster, PA 17603
(717) 392-8721

Hours: April-November: daily 10 AM-4:15 PM. Closed Thanksgiving. Candlelight tours in early December.

Cost: $5.50 adults, $4.50 seniors, $3.50 students, $1.75 ages 6-11, under 6 free.

Description: Eight-minute videotape introduces visitors to home of President James Buchanan. Well-informed guides in period costume add to the atmosphere. Children's tour available for this well-preserved mid-18th-century house.

Eating: Snack bar.

New Castle, Delaware

Settled in 1651 as a Dutch fort, this colonial riverfront town is a great half-day adventure with children. Wander through the quiet streets and into the historic buildings open to the public. Be sure to pick up a brochure which describes the history of the many private residences and public buildings. For information, call the Visitors Bureau at (800) 758-1550. Many exciting programs throughout the year.

Directions: I-95 South to exit 5A (New Castle) to Route 141 South. Follow signs into New Castle.

Amstel House—1738

4th and Delaware Streets
New Castle, DE 19720
(302) 322-2794

Hours: Tuesday-Saturday, 11 AM-4 PM; Sunday, 1 PM-4 PM. Closed on holidays.

Cost: $2.25 adults, $1.25 children ($4.00 combination ticket for Amstel House and Dutch House).

Description: This was thought to be the most elegant house in New Castle when it was built in 1738 and was the home of Governor Van Dyke. It's interesting to visit and compare this house with the Dutch House and will give kids a view of the difference in lifestyles in colonial times.

Court House—1732

Delaware Street
New Castle, DE 19720
(302) 323-4453

Hours: Tuesday-Saturday, 10 AM-3:30 PM; Sunday, 1:30 PM-4:30 PM. Closed on holidays.

Cost: Free.

Description: This was Delaware's colonial capitol and meeting place for the State Assembly until 1777. The court house tour will give you lots of interesting facts about the area. Be sure to climb to the cupola and learn how Delaware's northern boundary was established from that point!

Dutch House Museum—1700

4th Street
New Castle, DE 19720
(302) 322-9168

Hours: Tuesday-Saturday, 11 AM-4 PM; Sunday, 1 PM-4 PM. Closed on holidays.

Cost: $2.25 adults, $1.25 children ($4.00 combination ticket for Amstel House and Dutch House).

Description: A typical colonial house, this will fascinate all ages. The guide will show you the way those living in the house conserved space and used creative hiding places for many things.

George Read II's House—1801

42 The Strand
New Castle, DE 19720
(302) 322-8411

Hours: Tuesday-Saturday, 10 AM-4 PM; Sunday, 12 noon-4 PM. January-February: Weekdays by appointment only.

Cost: $4.00 adults, $3.50 seniors, $2.00 children 6-12, under 6 free.

Description: When it was built, this was the largest house in Delaware with 22 rooms. The gardens, established in 1847, are the oldest surviving gardens in the state. Still an impressive house to tour through.

New Jersey had its own "Tea Party" on the eve of the Revolutionary War, December 12, 1774.

The state bird of Pennsylvania is the ruffed grouse.

Working World

Children's curiosity about the working world turns any behind-the-scenes visit into an instant adventure. If you pick a time when the shop isn't crowded, most people are happy to explain their jobs to eager young listeners.

The organizations listed in this section offer official tours of varying lengths, but there are dozens of unlisted opportunities in every community. Don't forget to take the children to see your own places of work.

Chinatown

Between 8th and 11th Streets
Vine and Arch Streets
Philadelphia, PA 19107

Crayola Factory

See Museums, page 55

Cunningham Piano Company

5427 Germantown Avenue
Philadelphia, PA 19144
(215) 438-3200

Hours: Monday-Friday, tours at 10:30 AM or 1 PM. They are flexible, however, so call ahead if you want another time.

Cost: Free.

Description: A 1-hour tour gives visitors a chance to see craftsmen work on every stage of piano building, from design to construction and refinishing. Learn about the history of pianos and different styles.

Fabric Workshop

1315 Cherry Street
Philadelphia, PA 19107
(215) 568-1111

Hours: Monday-Friday, 9 AM-5 PM; Saturday, 12 noon-4 PM. Closed Saturdays in August.

Cost: Free. $1.00 donation recommended.

Description: Older students of textile art enjoy talking to artists at work and watching fabric being printed. Gallery on 5th floor. Large groups must call ahead.

Fire Stations

Local fire stations usually welcome young visitors, let them try on coats and helmets, climb on the engine, and clang the bell. Parents should call in advance to visit. Check local media for events planned around October Fire Prevention Week.

Free Library of Philadelphia

See Collections, page 60.

General Post Office

2970 Market Street
Philadelphia, PA 19104-9641
(215) 895-8000/8100

Hours: Tours: Monday-Friday, 10 AM. Call ahead to schedule.

Cost: Free.

Description: Detailed tour for ages 12 and up. See machinery, equipment, and lots of behind-the-scenes details. Requests for tours must be made in writing to Office of Communication, General Post Office, Philadelphia, PA 19104-9641. Children under 12 are encouraged to visit their *local* post office.

Time Needed: 1 hour.

Head House Square and New Market

2nd Street between Pine and Lombard Streets
Philadelphia, PA 19106

Description: Renovated Old Philadelphia marketplace. Busy in summer with many scheduled fairs and activities for all ages.

Herr's Snack Factory

Routes 1 and 272
P.O. Box 300
Nottingham, PA 19362
1-800-523-5030

Hours: Monday-Thursday, 9 AM-4 PM; Friday, 9 AM-12 noon.

Cost: Free.

(continued on next page)

Description: Tour takes you through the complete process of making potato chips, pretzels, and other snacks, from raw materials to finished products. No more than 10 people allowed on each tour, so it's best to call ahead for reservations.

Time Needed: 1 hour.

Eating: Free snack samples.

Driving: I-95 South to 322 West to Route 1 South to Nottingham exit 272. Turn left off ramp, go a quarter mile. Herr's is on the right.

Italian Market
9th Street, from Wharton to Christian Streets
Philadelphia, PA 19107

Description: Busy neighborhood bazaar packed with *everything* for sale.

KYW-TV 3
Independence Mall East
5th and Market Streets
Philadelphia, PA 19106
(215) 238-4905   &. 👕 🚐

Hours: Tuesday and Thursday, 9:30 AM-11:30 AM.

Cost: Free.

Description: If you call several weeks in advance, you can have a 45-minute tour of the television station, including studios, control rooms, weather station, and newsrooms. Maybe catch a glimpse of your favorite local newsperson.

Masonic Temple
See Glimpses of History, page 32.

New Jersey is the 46th largest state and could fit into Texas 37 times.

Moravian Pottery and Tile Works

130 Swamp Road (Route 313)
Doylestown, PA 18901
(215) 345-6722

Hours: Daily 10 AM-4:45 PM. Closed all major holidays.

Cost: $3.00 adults, $2.50 seniors, $1.50 children 6-17, under 6 free.

Description: 15-minute video, then self-guided tour. Watch tiles being made almost exactly as they were in 1900. Be sure to see Mercer Museum (page 65) and Fonthill (page 58) while in the area. Reservations requested.

Time Needed: 30-45 minutes.

Driving: I-95 North to Newtown, then take Route 413 North to Buckingham. Follow Route 202 North to Doylestown. Turn right onto Swamp Road (Route 313). Moravian is half a mile on left.

Newspapers

Local publications usually are pleased to give tours to groups that call ahead for reservations. Please do not call the Philadelphia newspapers.

Philadelphia International Airport

Division of Aviation
Terminal B, Philadelphia Airport
Philadelphia, PA 19153
(215) 937-6746

Hours: Monday-Friday, 10 AM-12 noon. Reservations required (10 person minimum, 30 person maximum).

Cost: Free.

Description: Get a tour of the operation of the entire airport, from ticketing to security checks to baggage handling. It is also possible to get a tour of the airfield on a specially marked bus.

Time Needed: 2 hours.

Tours/Programs: School groups welcome, 3rd grade and up.

Eating: Plenty throughout airport.

Pioneer Tunnel Coal Mine and Steam Locomotive
19th and Oak Streets
Ashland, PA 17921
(570) 875-3850

Hours: April, May, September, October: Mine tours: Monday-Friday, 11 AM, 12:30 PM, 2 PM; Saturday-Sunday, 10 AM-6 PM (closed weekends in April). Steam train rides: Monday-Friday, for groups by reservation only; Saturday-Sunday, 10 AM-6 PM (closed weekends in April). Memorial Day-Labor Day: Train rides and mine tours daily, 10 AM-6 PM.

Cost: Mine tours: $6.50 adults, $4.00 children under 12. Steam train: $4.50 adults, $3.00 children under 12.

Description: Restored coal mine lets you see how it once operated. Be sure to bring a jacket for the cold ride in an underground miner's car. Once inside the tunnel, you can get off while real coal miners explain the process. Steam locomotive ride goes around Mahonoy Mountain to a strip mine. Playground equipment next to tunnel. Anthracite Museum of Ashland nearby. Find your own fossils on the Fossil Site tour, arranged through tunnel office.

Time Needed: 1 1/2 hours.

Eating: Food stand and picnic tables near playground.

Driving: I-76 (Schuylkill Expressway) to Route 202 South to 422 West. Go through Pottstown, take Reading bypass to Route 61 North. Follow to Ashland.

Police Stations
With advance notice, most local police stations welcome young visitors. One group of youngsters we know got a tour of their local station, toy badges, bicycle safety stickers and rules, and a humbling chance to "be in jail."

PretzCo Soft Pretzel Bakery and Museum
312 Market Street
Philadelphia, PA 19106
(215) 413-3010

Hours: Monday-Saturday, 10 AM-4 PM.

Cost: $1.50 per person, includes a free soft pretzel.

(*continued on next page*)

Description: This is a perfect short outing. Watch a movie about the history of pretzels; go through the museum with its displays of old cooking facilities and different kinds of wheat; make your own pretzel in any shape you want. Then watch real pretzels being made in the bakery and taste their delicious varieties.

Tours/Programs: Make-your-own pretzels appeal to Scouts, birthday
parties, and school groups.

Reading Terminal Market
12th Street, from Market to Arch Streets
Philadelphia, PA 19107
(215) 922-2317, for market information

Description: Our country's only surviving single-span train shed is nearing 100 years old. No more trains but every imaginable kind of food. Children love to get ice cream, then wander around looking at whole fish, whole chickens, and area specialties.

Sturgis Pretzel House
See Lancaster, page 170.

Train Stations
From Philadelphia's giant 30th Street Station to the smallest local station, the fascination still holds for children. Most are content to just wander around, but for those who want to know more, ask the stationmaster to explain how the system works. For tours of 30th Street Station, call (215) 349-2153.

United States Courthouse
601 Market Street
Philadelphia, PA 19106
(215) 597-1897

Hours: Monday-Friday, 9 AM-4 PM, by reservation only.

Description: Sit in the gallery and see how a real trial works. This is not just "People's Court," so call ahead and let them help you pick a trial appropriate for your child's age and understanding. If you come with a school group, the judge may come over and talk to you at break time. Must be at least 9 years old.

Eating: Snack bar; cafeteria in Federal Building next door.

United States Mint

5th and Arch Streets
Philadelphia, PA 19106
(215) 408-0114   ♿ ✞ 🚌

Hours: September-April: Monday-Friday, 9 AM-4:30 PM; May-June: Monday-Saturday, 9 AM-4:30 PM; July-August: Monday-Sunday, 9 AM-4:30 PM.

Cost: Free.

Description: George Washington saw the need for a national system of coins, and he started the first mint just a few blocks from here. This is Philadelphia's fourth U.S. Mint building. Free brochure explains the exhibits as you go along. First part of building open to the public shows the history of coinage, second part lets visitors watch pieces of blank metal turn into coins. (No cameras or video equipment allowed.)

Time Needed: 1 hour.

Eating: None, but plenty of street vendors outside.

Workshop on the Water

See Independence Seaport Museum, page 63.

Helpful Phone Numbers

EMERGENCY AND HEALTH

Child Abuse Hotline (215) 683-6100
CONTACT (24-hour hotline) (215) 879-4402
Drug and Alcohol Abuse (800)-234-0420 or (215) 592-5451
Free Parent Counseling (215) 831-8855
Health Hotline 1-800-692-7254
Missing Children Hotline 1-800-843-5678
Poison Control Center (215) 386-2100
Runaway Hotline 1-800-231-6946
TEL-MED (215) 829-5500
Toy Safety Hotline 1-800-638-2772

PEDIATRIC HOSPITALS

Alfred I. DuPont Institute
Wilmington, DE
(302) 651-4000

Child Guidance Clinic
Philadelphia, PA
(215) 590-1000

Children's Hospital of Philadelphia
Philadelphia, PA
(215) 590-1000

Children's Rehabilitation Hospital
Thomas Jefferson Hospital
Philadelphia, PA
(215) 955-0606

Cooper Hospital
Camden, NJ
(609) 342-2001

St. Christopher's Hospital for Children
Philadelphia, PA
(215) 427-5000

Tourist Phone Numbers

Philadelphia

Independence National Historical Park Visitor Center
*   (215) 597-8974 or 627-1776*
Philadelphia Visitors Center (215) 636-1666
Time (215) 846-1212
Transportation:
    Amtrak transportation information (215) 824-1600
    PATCO high-speed line (215) 922-4600
    SEPTA transportation information (215) 580-7800
Traveler's Aid Society (215) 523-7580
Weather (215) WE6-1212

State Tourist Information Numbers

Delaware: 1-800-441-8846
New Jersey: 1-800-JERSEY-7
Pennsylvania: 1-800-847-4872

First-Choice Activities

Recommended by my own children, listed by county:

Delaware

New Castle
- Brandywine Zoo
- Delaware Toy and Miniature Museum
- Fort Delaware
- Hagley Museum and Eleutherian Mills
- Historic New Castle

New Jersey

Burlington
- Canoeing in the Pine Barrens

Camden
- Garden State Discovery Museum

Cumberland
- Historic Bridgeton
- Wheaton Village

Mercer
- New Jersey State Museum

Pennsylvania

Berks
- Crystal Cave
- Daniel Boone Homestead

Bucks
- Mercer Mile (Fonthill Museum, Mercer Museum, Moravian Pottery and Tile Works)
- Sesame Place

Chester
- Herr's Snack Factory
- Hopewell Furnace and Village
- Great Valley Nature Center
- Longwood Gardens

Dauphin
- Hershey attractions

Delaware
- Brandywine Battlefield State Park
- Colonial Pennsylvania Plantation

Lancaster
- Amish Homestead
- Discover Lancaster County History Museum
- Dutch Wonderland
- Pennsylvania Farm Museum of Landis Valley
- Strasburg Railroad and Railroad Museums
- Sturgis Pretzel House
- Weavertown One-Room Schoolhouse

Lehigh	Crayola Factory
Montgomery	Elmwood Park Zoo
	Valley Forge National Historic Park
Philadelphia	Annenberg Center Theater for Children
	Franklin Court
	Franklin Institute
	Insectarium
	"Kid's Corner," WXPN
	Masonic Temple
	Old Fort Mifflin
	Philadelphia Zoo
	Please Touch Museum
	Schuylkill Center for Environmental Education

Appendixes

APPENDIX A: FREE ACTIVITIES

Airdrie Forest Preserve

Anderson Bakery

Andorra Natural Area

Ashland Nature Center

Awbury Arboretum

Betsy Ross House

Brandywine Battlefield State Park

Briar Bush Nature Center

Bucks County Covered Bridges

Burlington County Historical Loops

Camden County Environmental Studies Center

Candy Americana Museum

Cape May County Park and Zoo

Carpenters Hall

Chocolate World

Churchville Nature Center

Cohanzick Zoo

Congress Hall

Cool Valley Preserve

Cunningham Piano

Declaration House

Delancey Street

Edgar Allan Poe National Historic Site

Elfreth's Alley Museum

Fire Stations

Fireman's Hall Museum

Founders Hall

Four Mills Nature Reserve

Fox Chase Farm

Franklin Court

Franklin Museum

Franklin's Bust

Freddy Hill Farms

Free Library of Philadelphia

General Post Office

George Lorimer Nature Preserve

German Society of Pennsylvania

Great Valley Nature Center

Grundy Museum

Gwynedd Wildlife Preserve

Hall of Fame Museum

Head House Square

Herr's Snack Factory

Historic Places of Worship

Historic Burlington County Prison-Museum

Historical Societies and Museums

Howell Living History Farm

Independence National Historical Park Visitors Center

Independence Hall

Jenkins Arboretum

John Heinz National Wildlife Refuge at Tinicum

"Kid's Corner" on WXPN

Kosciuszko National Memorial

KYW-TV 3

Laurel Hill Cemetery

Liberty Bell Pavilion

Marine Mammal Stranding Center

Masonic Temple

Mennonite Historians of Eastern Pennsylvania

Merrymead Farm

Mill Grove, Audubon Wildlife Sanctuary

Morton Homestead

Nail House Museum

New Hall Military Museum

New Jersey State Museum

Nolde Forest Environmental Education Center

North Museum of Franklin and Marshall College

Norview Farm

Old City Hall

Paley Design Center

Peace Valley Nature Center

Pennsylvania Hospital and Nursing Museum

Pennsylvania Hospital Physic Garden

Pennsylvania Dutch Visitors Bureau

Pennypack Environmental Nature Center

Pennypacker Mills

Peter Wentz Farmstead

Philadelphia Vietnam Veterans Memorial

Philadelphia International Airport

Phillips Mushroom Museum

Police Stations

Polish American Cultural Center Museum

Pool Wildlife Sanctuary

Potter's Tavern

Quaker Information Center

Rancocas Nature Center

Richard Allen Museum

Rickett's Circus

Riverbend Environmental Education Center

Robbins Park for Environmental Studies

Ryerss Museum

Ryerss' Farm for Aged Equines

Scott Arboretum of Swarthmore College

Second Bank of the United States

Silver Lake Nature Center

Smith Memorial Playgrounds & Playhouse

Springton Manor Farm

Sweden Farmstead Museum

Taylor Memorial Arboretum

Tomb of the Unknown Soldier

Train Stations

United States Courthouse

United States Mint

Upper Schuylkill Valley Park & Wildlife Center

Valley Forge National Historic Park

Wagner Free Institute of Science

Wagner Museum

Welkinweir Preserve

Woodruff Indian Museum

APPENDIX B: ACTIVITIES WITH FULL AND PARTIAL WHEELCHAIR AND STROLLER ACCESS

Academy of Natural Sciences

Afro-American Historical & Cultural Museum

Allentown Art Museum

American Helicopter Museum

Amish Country Homestead*

Amish Farm & House*

Amish Village

Ashland Nature Center of the Delaware Nature Society*

Atwater Kent Museum

Awbury Arboretum

Balch Institute for Ethnic Studies

Bartram's House and Gardens

Batsto Village*

Bowman's Hill

Boyertown Museum of Historical Vehicles

Brandywind Battlefield State Park

Brandywine Zoo

Brandywine River Museum & Conservancy

Briar Bush Nature Center*

Camden County Environmental Studies Center

Cape May County Park & Zoo

Carpenters Hall*

Childventure Museum

Chocolate World

Choo-Choo Barn

Churchville Nature Center

Clementon Amusement Park & Splashworld Water Park*

Cliveden

Cohanzick Zoo

Colonial Pennsylvania Plantation*

Colonial Flying Corps Museum

Congress Hall*

Conrad Weiser Homestead*

Cornwell Furnace*

Daniel Boone Homestead*

Declaration House*

Delaware Agricultural Museum

Delaware Art Museum

Delaware Museum of Natural History

Delaware Toy & Miniature Museum

Discover Lancaster County History Museum

Dorney Park & Wildwater Kingdom

Dutch Wonderland

Edgar Allan Poe Site*

Elmwood Park Zoo

Ephrata Cloister

Fabric Workshop

Fireman's Hall Museum

Folk Craft Center and Museum

Founders Hall

Four Mills Nature Reserve (Wissahickon Valley Watershed)*

Fox Chase Farm*

Franklin Court

Franklin Institute

indicates partial accessibility

Franklin Museum

Freddy Hill Farms

Free Library of Philadelphia

Garden State Discovery Museum

General Post Office*

George Read II House & Garden*

Germantown Historical Society Museum

Graeme Park*

Green Hills Farm*

Grundy Museum*

Hagley Museum & Eleutherian Mills*

Hall of Fame Sports Museum

Hands-on House

Hans Herr House

Hawk Mountain Sanctuary (Visitors Center)

Herr's Snack Factory

Hershey Gardens

Hershey Museum

Hersheypark

Hershey Visitors Center

Historic RittenhouseTown*

Hope Lodge & Mather Mill*

Hopewell Furnace & Village*

Horticulture Center

Howell Living History Farm*

Independence National Historical Park Visitor's Center

Independence Seaport Museum

Independence Hall*

Institute of Contemporary Art

James A. Michener Art Museum

John Heinz National Wildlife Refuge of Tinicum*

Kosciuszko National Memorial*

KYW-TV 3

Liberty Bell Pavilion

Library for the Blind & Physically Handicapped

Lights of Liberty

Longwood Gardens

Marine Mammal Stranding Center

Mary Merritt Doll Museum

Masonic Temple

Mennonite Heritage Center

Mercer Museum & Spruance Library*

Merrymead Farm*

Mill Bridge Village & Campground

Moravian Pottery & Tile Works*

Morris Arboretum of the University of Pennsylvania*

Mummers Museum

Mutter Museum of the College of Physicians*

Nail House Museum

National Museum of American Jewish History

New Jersey State Aquarium & Children's Garden

New Hall Military Museum*

New Jersey State Museum & Planetarium

Newlin Grist Mill Park*

Norman Rockwell Museum

North Museum of Franklin & Marshall College

Norview Farm*

Old Barracks Museum

Old City Hall

Old Fort Mifflin*

Paley Design Center

PAWS Farm Nature Center

Pennsbury Manor

Pennsylvania Academy of the Fine Arts

Pennsylvania Dutch Visitors Bureau

Pennsylvania Farm Museum of Landis Valley

Pennsylvania Hospital Physic Garden

Pennypacker Mills

Peter Wentz Farmstead*

Philadelphia International Airport

Philadelphia Museum of Art

Philadelphia Zoo

Phillips Mushroom Museum

Pioneer Tunnel Coal Mine & Steam Locomotive

Please Touch Museum

Pool Wildlife Sanctuary*

PretzCo Soft Pretzel Bakery & Museum

Pusey House & Landingford Plantation

Railroad Museum of Pennsylvania

Reading Public Museum and Art Gallery

Robbins Park for Environmental Studies*

Rock Ford Plantation & Kauffman Museum*

Rockwood*

Rodin Museum

Ryerss Museum

Ryerss' Farm for Aged Equines*

Schuylkill Center for Environmental Education

Scott Arboretum of Swarthmore College

Sesame Place

Six Flags Great Adventure

Smith Memorial Playgrounds & Playhouse*

Smithville

Springton Manor Farm

Stenton

Storybook Land

Sturgis Pretzel House

Sweden Farmstead Museum

Theaters (most)

Toy Train Museum

Trexler Lehigh Game Preserve

Tyler Arboretum*

United States Courthouse

United States Mint

University Museum of Archaeology & Anthropology

Upper Schuylkill Valley Park & Wildlife Center*

Valley Forge National Historic Park

Washington Crossing Historic Park*

Watch & Clock Museum of NAWCC

Weavertown One-Room Schoolhouse

Wetlands Institute*

Wharton Esherick Museum

Wheaton Village

Winterthur

Woodmere Art Museum

Woodruff Indian Museum

Zoo America

APPENDIX C: RAINY DAY OUTINGS

Academy of Natural Sciences

Afro-American Historical & Cultural Museum

Allentown Art Museum

American Helicopter Museum

American Swedish Historical Museum

Amish Country Homestead

Anderson Bakery

Andorra Natural Area

Atwater Kent Museum

Balch Institute for Ethnic Studies

Barnes-Brinton House

Batsto Village

Betsy Ross House

Boyertown Museum of Historical Vehicles

Brandywine River Museum & Conservancy

Briar Bush Nature Center

Brinton 1704 House

Camden County Environmental Studies Center

Candy Americana Museum/ Wilbur Chocolates

Carpenters Hall

Childventure Museum

Chocolate World

Choo-Choo Barn

Cliveden

Colonial Flying Corps Museum

Congress Hall

Cornwall Furnace

Crystal Cave

Cunningham Piano

Daniel Boone Homestead

Declaration House

Delaware Agricultural Museum

Delaware Art Museum

Delaware Museum of Natural History

Delaware Toy & Miniature Museum

Deshler-Morris House

Discover Lancaster County History Museum

Ebenezer Maxwell Mansion

Edgar Allan Poe National Historic Site

Ephrata Cloister

Fireman's Hall Museum

Folk Craft Center & Museum

Fonthill Museum

Founders Hall

Four Mills Nature Reserve (Wissahickon Valley Watershed)

Franklin Court

Franklin Institute

Franklin Museum

Free Library of Philadelphia

Garden State Discovery Museum

General Post Office

George Read II House & Garden

German Society of Pennsylvania

Germantown Historical Society Museum

Germantown Mennonite Historic Trust

Glencairn Museum

Graeme Park

Grange

Green Hills Farm

Grumblethorpe

Grundy Museum

Hall of Fame Sports Museum

Hands-on House

Hans Herr House

Herr's Snack Factory

Hershey Gardens

Hershey Museum

Hershey Park

Hershey Visitors Center

Historic RittenhouseTown

Historic Burlington County Prison-Museum

Historical Societies

Hope Lodge & Mather Mill

Horticultural Center

Howell Living History Farm

Independence Hall

Independence National Historical Park

Independence Seaport Museum

Insectarium

Institute of Contemporary Art

James A. Michener Art Museum

Japanese House & Garden

John Chads House

Johnson House

Kosciuszko National Memorial

KYW-TV 3

Liberty Bell Pavilion

Library for the Blind & Physically Handicapped

Longwood Gardens

Lost River Caverns

Mary Merritt Doll Museum

Masonic Temple

Massey House

Mennonite Heritage Center

Mercer Museum & Spruance Library

Moravian Pottery & Tile Works

Mummers Museum

Mutter Museum of the College of Physicians

Nail House Museum

National Musuem of American Jewish History

New Hall Military Museum

New Jersey State Aquarium & Children's Garden

New Jersey State Museum & Planetarium

Norman Rockwell Museum

North Museum of Franklin & Marshall College

Old Barracks Museum

Old City Hall

Old Dutch House

Paley Design Center

PAWS Farm Nature Center

Pennsylvania Academy of the Fine Arts

Pennsylvania Dutch Visitors Bureau

Pennsylvania Hospital & Nursing Museum

People's Place

Peter Wentz Farmstead

Philadelphia International Airport

Philadelphia Museum of Art

Philadelphia Zoo

Phillips Mushroom Museum

Pioneer Tunnel Coal Mine & Steam Locomotive

Please Touch Museum

Polish American Cultural Center Museum

Pool Wildlife Sanctuary

PretzCo Soft Pretzel Bakery & Museum

Pusey House & Landingford Plantation

Quaker Information Center

Railroad Museum of
Pennsylvania

Reading Public Museum
& Art Gallery

Richard Allen Museum

Robbins Park for
Environmental Studies

Rock Ford Plantation &
Kauffman Museum

Rockwood

Rodin Museum

Rosenbach Museum & Library

Ryerss Museum

Sanderson Museum

Schuylkill Center for
Environmental Education

Second Bank of the United
States

Smith Memorial Playgrounds
& Playhouse

Stenton

Sturgis Pretzel House

Theater Performances

Toy Train Museum

United States Mint

United States Courthouse

University Museum of
Archaeology &
Anthropology

Upsala

Valley Forge National
Historic Park

Wagner Free Institute
of Science

Washington Crossing
Historic Park

Watch & Clock Museum
of NAWCC

Weavertown One-Room
Schoolhouse

Wetlands Institute

Wharton Esherick Museum

Wheaton Village

Winterthur

Woodmere Art Museum

Woodruff Indian Museum

Wyck

APPENDIX D: ACTIVITIES FOR SCHOOL GROUPS

Academy of Natural Sciences

Afro-American Historical & Cultural Museum

Airdrie Forest Preserve

Allentown Art Museum

American Helicopter Museum

American Swedish Historical Museum

Amish Country Homestead

Amish Farm & House

Amish Village

Anderson Bakery

Andorra Natural Area

Ashland Nature Center of the Delaware Nature Society

Atwater Kent Museum

Awbury Arboretum

Balch Institute for Ethnic Studies

Barclay Farmstead

Barnes-Brinton House

Bartram's House & Gardens

Betsy Ross House

Bowman's Hill Wildflower Preserve

Boyertown Museum of Historical Vehicles

Brandywine Battlefield State Park

Brandywine Zoo

Brandywine River Museum & Conservancy

Briar Bush Nature Center

Brinton 1704 House

Camden County Environmental Studies Center

Candy Americana Museum

Cape May County Park & Zoo

Carpenters Hall

Childventure Museum

Chocolate World

Choo-Choo Barn

Churchville Nature Center

Cliveden

Cohanzick Zoo

Colonial Flying Corps Museum

Colonial Pennsylvania Plantation

Concord Schoolhouse

Congress Hall

Cool Valley Preserve

Cornwall Furnace

Crystal Cave

Cunningham Piano

Daniel Boone Homestead

Declaration House

Delaware Art Museum

Delaware Agricultural Museum

Delaware Museum of Natural History

Delaware Toy & Miniature Museum

Deshler-Morris House

Discover Lancaster County History Museum

Dutch Wonderland

Ebenezer Maxwell Mansion

Edgar Allan Poe National Historic Site

Elmwood Park Zoo

Ephrata Cloister

Fabric Workshop

Fireman's Hall Museum

Folk Craft Center and Museum

Fonthill Museum

Founders Hall

Four Mills Nature Reserve (Wissahickon Valley Watershed)

Fox Chase Farm

Franklin Institute

Franklin Museum

Franklin Court

Freddy Hill Farms

Free Library of Philadelphia

Garden State Discovery Museum

General Post Office

George Read II House & Garden

George Lorimer Nature Preserve

German Society of Pennsylvania

Germantown Mennonite Historic Trust

Germantown Historical Society Museum

Glencairn Museum

Graeme Park

Graff House

Grange

Great Valley Nature Center

Green Hills Farm

Grumblethorpe

Gwynedd Wildlife Preserve

Hagley Museum & Eleutherian Mills

Hands-on House

Hans Herr House

Hawk Mountain Sanctuary

Herr's Snack Factory

Hershey Gardens

Hershey Museum

Hersheypark

Hershey Visitors Center

Historic Burlington County Prison-Museum

Historic Fallsington Inc.

Historic RittenhouseTown

Hope Lodge & Mather Mill

Hopewell Furnace & Village

Howell Living History Farm

Independence Hall

Independence National Historical Park

Independence Seaport Museum

Insectarium

Institute of Contemporary Art

James A. Michener Art Museum

Japanese House & Garden

Jenkins Arboretum

John Chads House

John Heinz National Wildlife Refuge of Tinicum

Johnson House

Kosciuszko National Memorial

KYW-TV 3

Liberty Bell Pavilion

Library for the Blind & Physically Handicapped

Longwood Gardens

Lost River Caverns

Marine Mammal Stranding Center

Mary Merritt Doll Museum

Masonic Temple

Massey House

Mennonite Heritage Center

Mercer Museum & Spruance Library

Merrymead Farm

Mill Bridge Village & Campground

Mill Grove, Audubon Wildlife Sanctuary

Moravian Pottery & Tile Works

Morgan Loghouse

Morris Arboretum of the University of Pennsylvania

Morton Homestead

Mummers Museum

Mutter Museum of the College of Physicians

Nail House Museum

National Musuem of American Jewish History

New Hall Military Museum

New Jersey State Aquarium & Children's Garden

New Jersey State Museum & Planetarium

Newlin Grist Mill Park

Nolde Forest Environmental Education Center

Norman Rockwell Museum

North Museum of Franklin & Marshall College

Norview Farm

Old Barracks Museum

Old City Hall

Old Dutch House

Old Fort Mifflin

Paley Design Center

PAWS Farm Nature Center

Pennsbury Manor

Pennsylvania Academy of the Fine Arts

Pennsylvania Dutch Visitors Bureau

Pennsylvania Farm Museum of Landis Valley

Pennsylvania Hospital & Nursing Museum

Pennypack Environmental Center

Pennypacker Mills

People's Place

Peter Wentz Farmstead

Philadelphia International Airport

Philadelphia Museum of Art

Philadelphia Zoo

Phillips Mushroom Museum

Pioneer Tunnel Coal Mine & Steam Locomotive

Please Touch Museum

Polish American Cultural Center Museum

PretzCo Soft Pretzel Bakery & Museum

Quaker Information Center

Railroad Museum of Pennsylvania

Rancocas Nature Center

Reading Public Museum & Art Gallery

Richard Allen Museum

Riverbend Environmental Education Center

Robbins Park for Environmental Studies

Rock Ford Plantation & Kauffman Museum

Rockwood

Rodin Museum

Rosenbach Museum & Library

Ryerss' Farm for Aged Equines

Ryerss Museum

Sanderson Museum

Schuylkill Center for Environmental Education

Scott Arboretum of Swarthmore College

Second Bank of the United States

Sesame Place

Silver Lake Nature Center

Smith Memorial Playgrounds & Playhouse

Smithville

Springton Manor Farm

Stenton

Sturgis Pretzel House

Sweden Farmstead Museum

Taylor Memorial Arboretum

Theater Performances

Trexler Lehigh Game Preserve

Tyler Arboretum

United States Courthouse

United States Mint

University Museum of Archaeology & Anthropology

Upper Schuylkill Valley Park & Wildlife Center

Upsala

Valley Forge National Historic Park

Wagner Free Institute of Science

Washington Crossing Historic Park

Watch & Clock Museum of NAWCC

Weavertown One-Room Schoolhouse

Welkinweir Preserve

Wharton Esherick Museum

Wheatland

Wheaton Village

Winterthur

Woodmere Art Museum

Woodruff Indian Museum

Wyck

Zoo America

APPENDIX E: ACTIVITIES WITH MEMBERSHIP BENEFITS AND DISCOUNTS

Academy of Natural Sciences

Afro-American Historical & Cultural Museum

Allentown Art Museum

American Helicopter Museum

American Swedish Historical Museum

Andorra Natural Area

Ashland Nature Center of the Delaware Nature Society

Atwater Kent Museum

Balch Institute for Ethnic Studies

Barclay Farmstead

Barnes-Brinton House

Bartram's House & Gardens

Boyertown Museum of Historical Vehicles

Brandywine Battlefield State Park

Brandywine River Museum & Conservancy

Brandywine Zoo

Briar Bush Nature Center

Cape May County Park & Zoo

Cliveden

Cohanzick Zoo

Colonial Pennsylvania Plantation

Conrad Weiser Homestead

Cornwall Furnace

Daniel Boone Homestead

Delaware Agricultural Museum

Delaware Art Museum

Delaware Museum of Natural History

Delaware Toy & Miniature Museum

Elmwood Park Zoo

Fireman's Hall Museum

Fonthill Museum

Four Mills Nature Reserve (Wissahickon Valley Watershed)

Fox Chase Farm

Franklin Institute

Garden State Discovery Museum

George Read II House & Garden

German Society of Pennsylvania

Graeme Park

Great Valley Nature Center

Green Hills Farm

Hagley Museum & Eleutherian Mills

Hawk Mountain Sanctuary

Historic Burlington County Prison-Museum

Historic Fallsington Inc.

Hope Lodge & Mather Mill

Hopewell Furnace & Village

Howell Living History Farm

Independence Seaport Museum

James A. Michener Art Museum

John Chad House

Longwood Gardens

Massey House

Mercer Museum & Spruance Library

Mill Grove, Audubon Wildlife Sanctuary

Morris Arboretum of the University of Pennsylvania

Mummers Museum

New Jersey State Aquarium & Children's Garden

New Jersey State Museum & Planetarium

Old Barracks Museum

Old Dutch House

Old Fort Mifflin

Paley Design Center

PAWS Farm Nature Center

Peace Valley Nature Center

Pennsbury Manor

Pennsylvania Academy of the Fine Arts

Pennypack Environmental Center

Peter Wentz Farmstead

Philadelphia Museum of Art

Philadelphia Zoo

Please Touch Museum

Rancocas Nature Center

Reading Public Museum & Art Gallery

Robbins Park for Environmental Studies

Rock Ford Plantation & Kauffman Museum

Rockwood

Rosenbach Museum & Library

Schuylkill Center for Environmental Education

Scott Arboretum of Swarthmore College

Smithville

Springton Manor Farm

Tyler Arboretum

University Museum of Archaeology & Anthropology

Wagner Free Institute of Science

Washington Crossing Historic Park

Watch & Clock Museum of NAWCC

Wetlands Institute

Wharton Esherick Museum

Wheaton Village

Winterthur

Woodmere Art Museum

APPENDIX F: ACTIVITIES WITH BIRTHDAY PARTY FACILITIES

Academy of Natural Sciences

American Helicopter Museum

Andorra Natural Area

Ashland Nature Center of the Delaware Nature Society

Cape May County Park & Zoo

Childventure Museum

Cohanzick Zoo

Colonial Pennsylvania Plantation

Delaware Museum of Natural History

Dutch Wonderland

Elmwood Park Zoo

Four Mills Nature Reserve (Wissahickon Valley Watershed)

Franklin Institute

Freddy Hill Farms

Garden State Discovery Museum

Great Valley Nature Center

Hagley Museum & Eleutherian Mills

HersheyPark

Insectarium

James A. Michener Art Museum

Old Fort Mifflin

Mercer Museum & Spruance Library

Mummers Museum

New Jersey State Aquarium at Camden

PAWS Farm Nature Center

Philadelphia Zoo

Pioneer Tunnel Coal Mine & Steam Locomotive

Please Touch Museum

PretzCo Soft Pretzel Bakery & Museum

Riverbend Environmental Education Center

Rockwood

Sesame Place

Silver Lake Nature Center

Six Flags Great Adventure

Smith Memorial Playgrounds & Playhouse

Springton Manor Farm

Storybook Land

Trexler Lehigh Game Preserve

University Museum of Archaeology & Anthropology

Wetlands Institute

Wheatland

Zoo America

APPENDIX G: ACTIVITIES WITH SUMMER DAY CAMP PROGRAMS

Academy of Natural Sciences

Allentown Art Museum

American Helicopter Museum

Andorra Natural Area

Atwater Kent Museum

Barclay Farmstead

Briar Bush Nature Center

Brandywine Zoo

Cape May County Park & Zoo

Colonial Pennsylvania Plantation

Delaware Agricultural Museum

Delaware Museum of Natural History

Elmwood Park Zoo

Fonthill Museum

Four Mills Nature Reserve (Wissahickon Valley Watershed)

Franklin Institute

Garden State Discovery Museum

Great Valley Nature Center

Hagley Museum & Eleutherian Mills

Herr's Snack Factory

Hope Lodge & Mather Mill

James A. Michener Art Museum

Mercer Museum & Spruance Library

Moravian Pottery & Tile Works

New Jersey State Aquarium at Camden

New Jersey State Museum & Planetarium

Newlin Grist Mill Park

Old Dutch House

Pennsbury Manor

Pennsylvania Academy of the Fine Arts

Peter Wentz Farmstead

Philadelphia Zoo

Pioneer Tunnel Coal Mine & Steam Locomotive

People's Light & Theater Company

Riverbend Environmental Education Center

Rockwood

Silver Lake Nature Center

Wagner Free Institute of Science

Wetlands Institute

Winterthur

APPENDIX H: ACTIVITIES GROUPED BY COUNTY

DELAWARE

Kent County
Delaware Agricultural Museum

New Castle County
Amstel House

Ashland Nature Center

Brandywine Zoo

Coleman's Tree Farm

Court House

Delaware Art Museum

Delaware Children's Theatre

Delaware Museum of Natural History

Delaware Toy & Miniature Museum

Dutch House Museum

Flasky's Produce

George Read II House and Garden

Gerald Zeh Farm

Grand Opera House

Grand Slam USA

Hagley Museum and Eleutherian Mills

Historical Society of Delaware

Lovett Farms

Old Dutch House

Old Swedes Church

Playhouse Theater

Powell Farms

Pulaski's Product

Rockwood

Skating Club of Wilmington

Valley Brook Farm

Warner Enterprises

Wilderness Canoe Trips

Wilmington and Western Railroad

Winterthur

NEW JERSEY

Atlantic County
Batsto Village

Bel Haven Lake

Forks Landing Marina

Marine Mammal Stranding Center

Paradise Lakes Campground Canoe Rental

Storybook Land

Burlington County
Axten's Tree Farm

Beaver's Farm

Bud Wells Blueberries

Burlington County Cultural and Heritage Commission

Burlington County Historical Loop Tours

Burlington County Historical Society

Charles Wesner Farm

Chesterfield Tree Farm

Conte Farms

DeCou's Christmas Trees

Edward Wells Farm

Emmons Tree Farm

Evesham Skating Center

Fernbrook Farm Nursery

Four Winds Farm

Fred and III Farm

Giberson's Farm

Grand Slam USA

Gravely Pond

Griffin Farm

Haines Tree Farm

Historic Burlington County Prison Museum

Holiday Roller Skating Center
Indian Acres Tree Farm
Johnson's Corner Farm
Juliustown Tree Farm
Katona Farms
Kemlin Tree Farm
Mick's Canoe Rental
National Ballet of New Jersey
North Branch Blueberries
Orchard Lane Farm
PAWS Farm Nature Center
Performing Arts Center
Pine Barrens Canoe Rental
Piper Blueberry Farm
Rancocas Nature Center
Reeves Blueberry Farm
Riley's Tree Farm
River Side Homestead Farm
Robson Farm and Greenhouse
Russell Grover's Farm
Sharp Farm
Smithville
Springville Orchard
Strawberry Hill Farm
Tom Haines Blueberries
Train Tree Plantation
Wading Pines Campgrounds
Wading River Christmas
    Tree Farm
Warren Ash Farm
Worrell Blueberries
Worth & Sharp Christmas
    Tree Farm

Camden County
Barclay Farmstead
Brown Tree Farm
Camarata Opera Theatre
Camden County
    Environmental
    Studies Center

Camden County Historical
    Society
Cherry Hill Skating Center
Clementon Amusement Park
Coliseum Skating Rink
Echelon Skating Center
Garden State Discovery
    Museum
Haddonfield Plays and Players
Haddonfield Symphony
New Jersey State Aquarium
    & Children's Garden
Peter P. Lucca Farm
Puttin' on the Ritz Children's
    Theatre
Springdale Farms
Vertical Reality
Village Players of Hatboro
Walt Whitman Cultural
    Arts Center

Cape May County
Cape May County Park and Zoo
Island Kayaks
TI Kayaks
Wetlands Institute

Cumberland County
Bridgeton
Bridgeton Theatre in the Park
Bridgeton Walking Tour
Cohanzick Zoo
Hall of Fame Sports Museum
McDermott's Christmas Trees
Nail House Museum
Nate Bisconte Farm
Sidney Rassas Farm
South Jersey Wheelmen
Sweden Farmstead Museum
Wheaton Village
Woodruff Indian Museum

Gloucester County
Belly Acres Christmas Trees
Cedarvale Farms
Cowtown Rodeo
Deptford Skating Center
Duffield's Farm Market
Exley's Country Lane Nursery
Franklin Skating Center
Fruitwood Orchards
Gloucester County Historical
   Society
Grace Christmas Tree Farm
Gypsy Run Tree Farm
Hank's Christmas Tree Ranch
LB's Trees
Mood's Farm Market
Patane's Farm
Pek's Trees
Robert's Nursery
Stecher's Country Store
Triple Oaks Nursery
Tuck-A-Lou Orchards
U-Pick

Mercer County
Bear Swamp Christmas
   Tree Farm
Grover Farm
Howell Living History Farm
Lee Turkey Farm
New Jersey State Museum and
   Planetarium
Old Barracks Museum
Terhune Orchards
Tindall Farm
War Memorial Theater

Ocean County
Six Flags Great Adventure

Salem County
Appel Farm Arts
Daniel L. Sauder Farm

Larchmont Farms
Nichols Orchards
Ralph Battle Farm
Stimpson's Tree Farm
William Jenkins Farm

PENNSYLVANIA
Berks County
Berks County Historical
   Society
Blue Mountain and Reading
   Railroad
Boyertown Museum of
   Historic Vehicles
Conrad Weiser Homestead
Cornwall Furnace
Crystal Cave
Daniel Boone Homestead
Grand Slam USA
Hawk Mountain Sanctuary
Mary Merrill Doll Museum
Merritt's Museum of
   Childhood
Nolde Forest Environmental
   Education Center
Reading Public Museum, Art
   Gallery and Planetarium
W.K. & S. Railroad

Bucks County
Bowman's Hill Wildflower
   Preserve
Bristol Riverside Theater
Bryan's Farm
Bucks County Carriages
Bucks County Covered Bridges
Bucks County Historical
   Society
Bucks County Community
   College Theater
Bucks County Playhouse
Bucks County River Country
Churchville Nature Center

Cornwell's Roller Skating Center

Evergreen Christmas Tree Farm

Evergreenery

Face-Off Circle

Fairview Farms

Fisher's Christmas Tree Farm

Fonthill Museum

Ghost Tours

Gold Mine Christmas Tree Farm

Grand Slam USA

Green Hills Farm

Grundy Museum

Historic Fallsington

Holiday Christmas Tree Farm

Indian Walk Tree Farm

Jacob & Jayne Wildemore

James A. Michener Art Museum

McArdle Tree Farm

Mercer Museum and Spruance Library

Moravian Pottery and Tile Works

New Hope Mule Barge

None Such Farm

Our Lady of Czestochowa

Peace Valley Nature Center

Pennsbury Manor

Penn Vermont Fruit Farms

Pine Tree Farm

Rollerama Skating Center

Rushton Tree Farm

Sesame Place

Shady Brook Farm

Shelly and Hellerick Farm

Silver Lake Nature Center

Snipes Farm

Solly Brothers Market

Tinicum Village Tree Farm

Top of the Hill Farm

Trauger's Farm Market

Tryon Farm

Tuckamony Farm

Wagner Museum

Warwick Twin Rinks

Washington Crossing Historic Park

Watson Tree Farm

Weber Farm

Winterberry Christmas Tree Farm

Carbon County

Blue Mountain Ski Area

Chester County

Air Ventures

Airdrie Forest Preserve

American Helicopter Museum

American Heritage Landmark Tours

Balloonair

Barnard's Orchards

Barns-Brinton House

Bernard's Tree Farm

Brandywine Battlefield State Park

Brandywine River Museum and Conservancy

Brandywine Valley Association

Brinton 1704 House

Caln Miniature Golf

Chadds Peak

Chester County Historical Society

Chester Springs Tree Farm

Colonial Flying Corps Museum

Cool Valley Preserve

Farmer in Lyndell

Footlighters Theater
Forge Theater
Gateway Stables
George Lorimer Nature Preserve
Grand Slam USA
Great Valley Nature Center
Great Valley Stables
Grigson Farm
Herr's Snack Factory
Highland Orchards
High's Nursery
Hopewell Furnace and Village
Horizon's Balloon Team
Immaculata College Theater
Irish Green Nursery
Jenkins Arboretum
John Chads House
Lollipop Balloon
Longwood Gardens
Magical Mystery Flights
Malickson's Tree Farm
Milky Way Farm
Northbrook Canoe
Northbrook Orchards
Nussex Farms
People's Light and Theater Company
Phillips Mushroom Museum
Pine Hill Farm
Pond View Tree Farm
Pusey House and Landingford Plantation
Ryerss' Farm for Aged Equines
Sanderson Museum
Shamrock Tree Farm
Sheeder Mill Farm
Springton Manor Farm
Stubles' Christmas Trees
Sugartown Strawberries
Valley Forge Historical Society

Valley Forge Music Fair/Children's Musical Theater
Valley Forge National Historic Park
Vertical Extreme
Welkinweir Preserve
West Chester and Barleysheaf Players
Wharton Esherick Museum
Windridge Farm
Windswept Farm
Yeager's Farm

Dauphin County
Chocolate World
Hershey
Hershey Gardens
Hershey Museum of American Life
Hershey Park
Middletown & Hummelstown Railroad
Zoo America

Delaware County
Cabrini College Theater
Colonial Pennsylvania Plantation
Delaware County Historical Society
Eastern College Planetarium and Observatory
Family Fun Spot
Franklin Museum
Grand Slam USA
Grange
Hedgerow Theater
Indian Orchards
Linvilla Orchards
Marple Newtown Historical Society
Marple Newtown Players
Massey House

Meagher Theater

Media Theatre for the Performing Arts

Morton Homestead

Newlin Grist Mill Park

Pusey House & Landingford Plantation

Putt Putt Golf Course

Radnor Historical Society

Ridley Creek State Park

Scott Arboretum

Skatium

Smallbrook Farm Evergreen Nursery

Sproul Observatory

Taylor Memorial Arboretum

Tyler Arboretum

Upper Darby Performing Arts Center

Villanova Observatory

Villanova Skating Arena

Lackawanna County
Montage Ski Area

Red Baron's Games

Lancaster County
Abe's Buggy Rides

Amish Country Homestead

Amish Experience

Amish Farm and House

Amish Village

Anderson Bakery

Candy Americana Museum

Choo-Choo Barn

Discover Lancaster County History Museum

Dutch Wonderland

Eagle Falls

Ed's Buggy Rides

Ephrata Cloisters

Folk Craft Center and Museum

Forest Ridge Stables

Fulton Opera House

Hands-on House

Hans Herr House

Kitchen Kettle Village

Lancaster County Heritage Center

Lancaster Newspaper Newseum

Mennonite Heritage Center

Mill Bridge Village

North Museum, Franklin and Marshall

Pennsylvania Dutch Visitors Bureau

Pennsylvania Farm Museum of Landis Valley

People's Place

Railroad Museum of Pennsylvania

Rock Ford Plantation of Kauffman Museum

Strasburg Railroad

Sturgis Pretzel House

Toy Train Museum

Watch and Clock Museum of the NAWCC

Weavertown One-Room Schoolhouse

Wheatland

Lehigh County
Allentown Art Museum

Canal Boat Rides

Crayola Factory

Doe Mountain Ski Area

Dorney Park/Wildwater Kingdom

Grand Slam USA

Kohler's Tree Farm

Lehigh County Historical Society

Pool Wildlife Sanctuary

Strawberry Acres

Trexler Lehigh Game Preserve

Luzerne County

Big Boulder Ski Area

Jack Frost Ski Area

Lehigh Rafting Rentals

Split Rock Ski Area

Lycoming County

Crystal Cave

Monroe County

Alpine Mountain

Camelback Ski Area

Shawnee Ski Area

Montgomery County

Ashford Farms

Beth Shalom Synagogue

Boswell's Tree Farm

Briar Bush Nature Center

Bryn Athyn Swedenborgian
Cathedral

Buck Nursery

Childventure

Elmwood Park Zoo

F & H Tree Farm

Four Mills Nature Reserve

Freddy Hill Farms

General Washington
Recreation Rink

Glencairn Museum

Graeme Park

Gwynedd Wildlife Preserve

Hague's Christmas Trees

Haverford College
Observatory

Hope Lodge and Mather Mill

Keswick Theater

Merrymead Farm

Mill Grove, Audubon Wildlife
Sanctuary

Montgomery County

Community College
Theater

Montgomery County
Historical Museum

Morgan Loghouse

New Hope Steam Railway

Norview Farm

Old York Road Skating Club

Pennypacker Mills

Peter Wentz Farmstead

Philadelphia Rock Gym

Ryerss Home for Aged
Equines

Riverbend Environmental
Education Center

Robbins Park for
Environmental Education

S-Berry Farm

Scottish Historic and Research
Society of Delaware Valley

Spring Mountain Ski Area

Storybook Musical Theatre

Tom's Trees

Upper Schuylkill Valley Park
and Wildlife Center

U.S. Naval Air Station,
Willow Grove

Valley Forge National
Historic Park

Varner's Tree Farm

Viking Ice Arena

Wagner Museum

Winter Sport Ice Arena

Northampton County

Lost River Caverns

Philadelphia County

Academy of Natural Sciences

Afro-American Historical
and Cultural Museum

Al Albert's Showcase

American Family Theater

American Heritage Landmark Tours

American Swedish Historical Museum

American Theater Arts for Youth

American Youth Hostels

Andorra Natural Area

Annenburg Center Theater for Children

Arthur Ashe Youth Tennis Center

Atwater Kent Museum

Awbury Arboretum

Balch Institute

Bartram's House and Gardens

Belmont Mansion

Betsy Ross House

Bicycle Club of Philadelphia

Bicycle Coalition

Black History Strolls

Burholme Golf

Byrne Golf Course

Carman Gardens Roller Skating Rink

Carpenters Hall

Cathedral Basilica of Saints Peter and Paul

Cathedral of the Immaculate Conception

Cedar Grove

Centipede Tours

Chamounix Youth Hostel

Cheltenham Playhouse Children's Theater

Children's Italian Market Tours

Choo-Choo Trolley

Christ Church

Civil War Library and Museum

Class of 1923 Rink

Cliveden

Cobbs Creek Golf Course

Cobbs Creek Rink

Concord Schoolhouse

Congress Hall

Conwell Dance Theater

Cunningham Piano Co.

Cycling Enthusiasts of the Delaware Valley

Declaration House

Delancey Street

Deshler-Morris House

Eagles Games

Eastern State Penitentiary

Ebenezer Maxwell Mansion

Edgar Allan Poe National Historic Site

Elfreth's Alley and Museum

Elmwood Roller Skating Rink

Fabric Workshop

Fairmount Park

Fairmount Park Bike Rentals

Fairmount Park Houses

Fels Planetarium

Fireman's Hall Museum

Flyers Games

Fox Chase Farm

Franklin Court

Franklin Institute and Fels Planetarium

Franklin's Bust

Free Library of Philadelphia

Gazela of Philadelphia

General Post Office of Philadelphia

German Society of Pennsylvania

Germantown

Germantown Historical Society Museum

Germantown Mennonite Historic Trust

Philadelphia Orchestra's
  Family Concerts
Philadelphia Tours
Philadelphia Vietnam Veterans
  Memorial
Philadelphia Visitors Center
Philadelphia Zoo
Phillies Games
Plays and Players Children's
  Theater
Please Touch Museum
Please Touch/Virginia
  Evans Theater
Polish American Cultural
  Center Museum
PretzCo
Quaker Information Center
Reading Terminal Market
Richard Allen Museum
Rickett's Circus
Riverlink Ferry
RiverRink
Rizzo Rink
Rodin Museum
Ronald MacDonald
  Children's Theater
Roosevelt Golf Course
Rosenbach Museum and
  Library
Ryerss Museum
St. Peter's Episcopal Church
Schuylkill Center for
  Environmental
  Education
Second Bank of the
  United States
Settlement Music School
  Recitals
76 Carriage Company
76ers Games
Simon's Skating Rink

Smith Memorial Playgrounds
  and Playhouse
Society Hill Carriage Company
Spirit of Philadelphia
Stenton
Strawberry Mansion
Sweetbriar Mansion
Temple University's Conwell
  Dance Theater
Tomb of the Unknown Soldier
United States Courthouse
United States Mint
University Museum of
  Archaeology and
  Anthropology
Upsala
US Golf
USS Becuna
USS Olympia
Wagner Free Institute
  of Science
Walnut Lane Golf Course
Wings Games
Wissahickon Ice Skating Club
Wistar Institute Museum
Woodford Mansion
Woodmere Art Museum
Wyck

Pike County
Camp Speers Ski Area

Schuylkill County
Pioneer Tunnel Coal Mine and
  Steam Locomotive

Sullivan County
Hanley's Happy Hill Ski Area

Susquehanna County
Elk Mountain Ski Area

Union County
Ski Roundtop

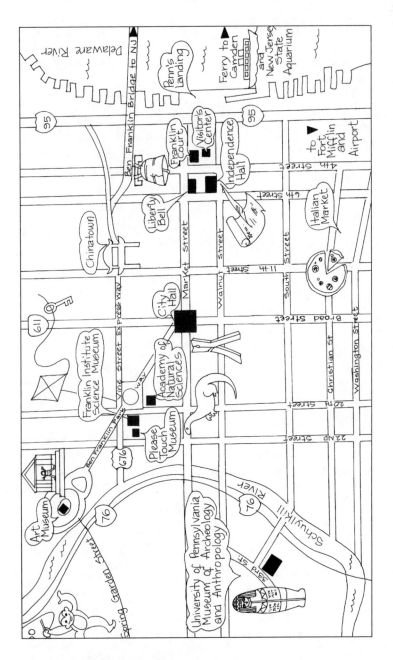

Center City Philadelphia

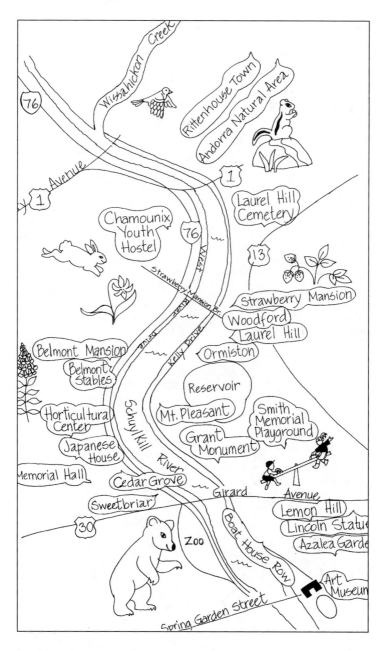

Fairmount Park

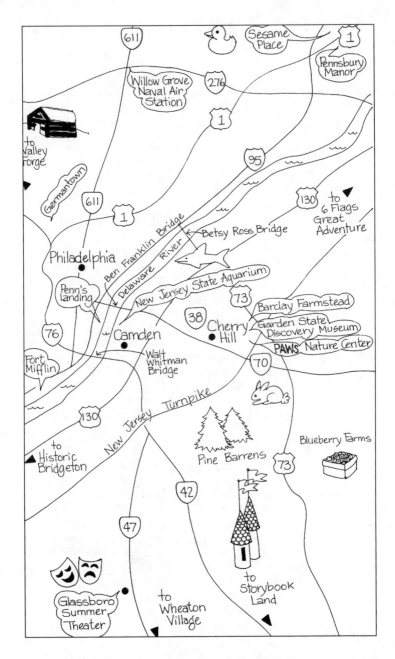

Southeastern Pennsylvania and New Jersey

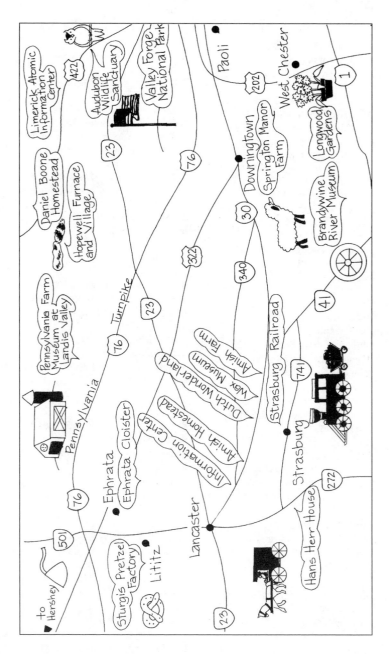

Paoli to Lancaster

Index

T

U

Elizabeth S. Gephart, a former teacher and mother of three, is a creative and resourceful Philadelphian who grew up and was educated in the Delaware Valley.

Notes

Notes

Notes

Notes